TOPIARY
AND THE ART OF
TRAINING PLANTS

TOPIARY
AND THE ART OF TRAINING PLANTS

DAVID JOYCE

FIREFLY BOOKS

This book is dedicated to the memory of
ELIZABETH ANNE HICKEY
RUA MAY JOYCE

A FIREFLY BOOK

Published by Firefly Books Ltd, 2000

Topiary and the Art of Training Plants
Copyright © Frances Lincoln Limited 2000
Text and garden designs copyright
© David Joyce 1999
Photographs copyright © as in
acknowledgments page 160
Garden plans by Laura Stoddart
and all other artwork by Clare Roberts
copyright © Frances Lincoln 2000
First Printing

Library of Congress Cataloguing in
Publication Data is available

Canadian Cataloguing in Publication Data
Joyce, David
Topiary and the art of training plants
Includes index.
ISBN 1-55209-420-0 (bound)
ISBN 1-55209-422-7 (pbk.)
1. Topiary work. 2. Ornamental climbing
plants — Training. I. Stoddart, Laura.
II. Title.
SB463.J69 2000 715 .1 C99-930375-9

Topiary and the Art of Training Plants
was edited, designed and produced by
Frances Lincoln Ltd
4 Torriano Mews
Torriano Avenue
London NW5 2RZ
Set in Van Dijck by
Frances Lincoln Limited
Printed and bound in Singapore

Published in the United States in 2000 by
Firefly Books (U.S.) Inc.
PO Box 1338, Ellicott Station
Buffalo, New York 14205

Published in Canada in 2000 by
Firefly Books Ltd.
3680 Victoria Park Avenue
Willowdale, Ontario M2H 3K1

TITLE PAGE ILLUSTRATION:
The solidity of topiary is widely
used to provide a contrast to the
loose shapes of roses. The strong lines of
this layout are emphasized by the avenue
of boxwood balls, contrasts of light and
shade adding to the weight of the shapes.
Paired arrangements, commonly used to
frame focal points or to mark the
junctions of paths, are a simple
way of underlining formal layouts.

Contents

Introduction

The shaping of bushes by browsing animals perhaps provides a clue to the original inspiration for topiary. Shrubby evergreen oaks constantly nibbled by goats on the dry hillsides of southern Europe and heathland gorse relentlessly grazed by a dense population of rabbits, for instance, form curious assemblies of near-symmetrical or bizarre shapes, all the more fantastic when tufts that animals find difficult to reach have continued to grow freely. Or perhaps no such inspiration was needed, for very early representations of plants in Ancient Egypt and the Middle East show trees and shrubs of symmetrical shape planted in ordered rows; so it is possible that the models for topiary, at least that of geometric character, were trees of very regular growth such as Italian cypresses (*Cupressus sempervirens*). After visiting the Giardino dei Giusti in Verona and seeing "monstrous cypresses, all pointed up like spikes into the air," the German poet Goethe noted that "the Taxus [yew], which in northern gardening we find cut to a sharp point, is probably

an imitation of this splendid natural product" (September 1786, *Travels in Italy*). Contrasting with this tradition of topiary, which despite its geometric nature often has an arbitrariness in its shapes, is another tradition of training and pruning, which has a long history in the East. In the Japanese craft of bonsai, specialized techniques result in scaled-down and idealized versions of trees and shrubs conforming to a strictly codified aesthetic.

It was Roman gardeners in the 1st century A.D. who first developed the shaping of trees and shrubs by regular trimming into a garden craft. Topiary entered the mainstream of European gardening when Italian Renaissance gardeners turned back to Ancient Rome and Greece for ideas. Topiary was only one element in the gardening legacy inherited from the Classical world, which Renaissance gardeners set in the broad context of formal layouts, usually terraced and divided into compartments, alive with the sound of moving water, populated with the gods of pagan

LEFT Simple geometric shapes, sometimes in combination, are still today, as they have been since Roman times, a major part of the topiary repertoire. A background of dark yew hedges intensifies the radiance of a block and ball shaped out of golden privet.

OPPOSITE Topiary, formal hedges and other kinds of plant training are strongly associated with the squared and symmetrical layouts that are the legacy of Renaissance and Baroque gardens. However, a more relaxed approach to the use of shaped plants is possible, as is shown in the curving lines of these boxwood hedges and the placing of a standard rose and topiary cones in an informally planted border.

LEFT Beech is deciduous but, like hornbeam, when it is clipped the dead leaves are retained through the winter. The warm color of these beech hedges contrasts with the green of geometric boxwod shapes and of the distant bird topiary.

OPPOSITE The qualities that make good hedging and topiary plants are found in a relatively small number of evergreens. The common boxwood, known to the Romans, remains a classic plant for low hedges and medium-size topiary. It is tolerant of many conditions and forms a dense surface when clipped; its relatively slow growth means that its shape holds well, even with only one trim a year. Here a circular walk bordered on both sides by pleached lindens is edged on one side by a low boxwood hedge and on the other by rounded topiary shapes in boxwood.

mythology, and generously planted with trees and shrubs in neat order. The living sculpture and architecture, sometimes richly patterned, that derive from this tradition of gardening form the subject of this book.

The formal garden in the Renaissance mold, with its appealing echoes of the Ancient world, has played such a dominant role in the history of European gardens that it may take a leap of the imagination to realize that its components—including topiary, hedges and patterned layouts—have an independent existence. An important aim of this book is to encourage gardeners to see that this gardening vocabulary can be used—in large and small gardens, in overall schemes or as single statements—with zestful freshness as well as in traditional ways.

In praise of trimmed plants

The fashionable revival of interest in topiary and other components of formal gardens allows us to see what have always been their strong points. One of these is weight. Topiary and hedges give a reassuring impression of established order and permanence in the garden that is difficult to achieve in any other way, except by stone and brick masonry. An assembly of formal components can create a garden of calm solemnity; and topiary and hedges also combine well with the more ephemeral effects of color and texture. Living sculpture and architecture have their own seasonal changes, an attractive moment being when new growth threatens to obscure clipped shapes. But at its best the year-round framework of green needs no floral titillation in spring and summer

to give it value. And, if the layout has been thoughtfully designed, green architecture works well with real architecture, extending the lines of buildings and completing vistas.

In this respect formal gardens show remarkable adaptability. In the past they have often been seen as mediating between the house and the landscape beyond, whether looking out on an Italian view of hills and valleys or, in a grand French garden, framing perspectives that seem to extend to infinity; but the reality for many gardeners is that the best chance of making something worthwhile of a small to medium-size urban plot is to avoid making connections with the world beyond. To do this, a self-contained design is needed, its internal structure working even when it is fully enclosed. Hedges and other living screens of the formal

garden create the shelter and privacy that make a little paradise possible, and topiary or patterned planting can ensure that the garden has a satisfying internal dynamic. The combination of hedged compartments and topiary can provide the basis for some of the simplest and most pleasing designs for small gardens, while container-grown topiary and trained plants are versatile garden components for paved yards or patios and balconies.

Gardeners who have never attempted topiary often feel that mysterious and labor-intensive techniques are involved in forming a shape that may take many years to reach maturity. This is not so. The only really essential requirement is a little self-confidence. The few techniques involved are simple and within the competence of inexperienced gardeners. The plants most commonly used are

LEFT Boxwood topiary near the door and arc-like hedges set in grass seem to be a simplified version of a parterre that may once have filled the terrace of this French château.

OPPOSITE Ornamental citrus trees are set out in a pattern of dwarf boxwood hedges at Herrenhausen, formerly a summer residence of the Electors of Hanover, Lower Saxony. In the 17th century, grand French gardens were models for many European gardens; but another influence was the more intimate style developed in the Netherlands, felt particularly at Herrenhausen, as Sophie, wife of the Elector Ernst August, who created the garden, grew up in the Netherlands and her gardener had been trained there.

remarkably tough, and with good sharp tools all the clipping is light easy work. Furthermore, topiary is not time-consuming to look after. In the formative stages and even when the shapes are mature, simple cones and pyramids under 6ft (1.8m) high can normally be clipped in five minutes or less. A satisfying small-scale shape can be achieved in a few years. And almost everyone who has trained and maintained topiary speaks of the formative pruning and subsequent clipping as a pleasurable and highly satisfying activity.

Hedges, knots and embroidered patterns are inevitably more time-consuming to look after. They are not intrinsically difficult to lay out and, provided the plants used are slow-growing—such as boxwood (*Buxus sempervirens*) and yew (*Taxus baccata*)—there is only one major burst of activity a year. With powered hedge-trimmers even long hedges can be clipped quite quickly, but the maintenance should be planned before planting on a grand scale. Working from ladders and platforms or trimming detailing of any kind add considerably to the time it takes to cut hedges.

The important thing is to be aware of how much effort is required for each technique and attempt only those that suit you. Whether you try a boxwod cone or a yew tunnel, the potential rewards are considerable. Gardeners of different tastes find in topiary, and in the use of hedges and patterned planting, a way of creating something of marked individuality, even when the formula has been used so often before. Countless variations are possible in the arrangement of geometric shapes and in the weave and flow of patterns. For many gardeners, however, the great delight of topiary is the possibility of expressing their own lighthearted fantasies in a sympathetic, easily worked medium. The models of the past remain a major source of inspiration for gardens today, but the scope for innovation in the treatment of space and juxtaposition of familiar and unfamiliar abstract shapes gives topiary and the use of hedges and patterned planting an exciting future.

The historical perspective

Renaissance and Baroque gardens have so powerfully defined the role of topiary and shaped plants that it is easy to overlook the horticultural techniques employed in medieval gardens. Illustrations in late medieval manuscripts show gardens divided into small compartments by walls, hedges and fences of palings, trellis or wattle; the trellis and wattle fences usually support climbing roses, grapevines or honeysuckle. Within the compartments, raised beds are often planted with trained shrubs. The *estrade*, a shrub trained in tiers, usually on wheel-like supports of metal or wood, is particularly associated with the Burgundian style of the 15th century. There were also more fanciful frames, outlining, for example, little ships and double crowns. The major architectural components consisted of arbors and tunnel arbors made of wood and withies which, planted with climbers like those trained on trellis and wattle fences, provided shaded areas for sitting outdoors and for walking.

As can be seen from a famous set of lunettes executed by Giusto Utens between 1599 and 1602, depicting estates in the vicinity of Florence, the gardens of small properties in 16th-century Tuscany were often highly conservative in their arrangement of compartments and shaped plants. But here, as elsewhere in Italy, there is striking evidence of garden architects imposing an overall design on the terrain, with vistas extending through and beyond the terraced gardens ensuring that landscape, garden and villa or palazzo all related to one another. In the gardens that survive, such as Villa Lante at Bagnaia or, the most famous of all, Villa d'Este at Tivoli, changes of fashion, the aging of trees and shrubs, the thickening of old topiary and hedges and simple decay now obscure the original conception. The once trim and clean lines underlying the romantically melancholic fullness of the gardens in their present state are best appreciated by turning to old engravings, paintings and frescoes. It is then possible to get some idea of the contrasts that were intended: between architecture and plants; still and moving water; open or public areas and the intimate *giardino segreto* or the mysterious grotto; plain green and the color of flowers or the fruits of citrus trees; ordered garden and unstructured landscape; and the informal growth of *boschi* (groves) of ever-

green oaks (*Quercus ilex*) and the geometry of shaped plants. The trimmed topiary, neatly hedged compartments, simple patterns in boxwood and ambitious mazes or green theaters of Italian gardens have inspired imitation in more northern gardens.

In the England of Elizabeth I and even in the reign of James I, when Continental influences were felt more strongly, no gardens were designed with a sophistication to match the assured examples of 16th-century Italy. There was, however, considerable interest in gardening, which extended below royal and aristocratic levels of society to the owners of small estates. The shaping of shrubs and trees, the organization of the grounds in compartments and ordered planting all made a sharp distinction between garden and nature. The enclosed, inward-looking character of the gardens is seen in the intricate pattern of knots, typically laid in quarters, each compartment planted with a geometric design of interweaving lines, usually incorporating topiary. The domestic scale

and regularity of the knot garden, not to mention its adaptability to sites where the genius of the place has long since fled, make it one of the most appealing of historic garden features to recreate. There is a curious attitude toward it that goes beyond fascination with history to a harmless but sometimes precious nostalgia for a supposed golden age, before Western gardens were filled with plant introductions from every corner of the world.

French gardens illustrated in the two volumes of Jacques Androuet du Cerceau's *Les plus excellents bastiments de France*, published between 1576 and 1579, reveal important sources of inspiration for some of the major gardens in England in the 16th century. The gardens illustrated, such as those at Blois, were impressive in their scale, but their character was conservative, the major features being geometrically patterned compartments and covered galleries. The geometric pattern of the Jardin Potager at Villandry, Indre-et-Loire, is directly inspired by engravings by du Cerceau. This richly symbolic garden, one of the most astonishing recreations of a period garden this century, was created between 1906 and 1924 by Dr Joachim Carvallo on three levels, with a Jardin d'Ornement, a Jardin Potager and a Jardin d'Eau. Magnificently maintained, the garden is full of details of trained plants that can be translated into modest-size gardens.

In the gardens illustrated by du Cerceau there is barely a hint of the originality and magnificence that was to characterize French gardens during the reign of Louis XIV. The hierarchy of components within the regularized plan of the classic French garden—*parterres de broderie* (embroidered parterres) nearest the château, *bosquets* (groves) pierced by walks more distant—were clearly formulated in the mid-17th century by André Mollet, in his publication *Le Jardin de plaisir*. The transformation of theory into gardens of heroic scale but subtle detail was largely the work

of the landscape architect André Le Nôtre. His first great success was for Nicolas Fouquet at Vaux-le-Vicomte, much of which has been restored. Subsequently, under the patronage of Louis XIV, he was largely responsible for the major development of the royal gardens at Versailles. The stupendous resources made available are evidence of the importance the garden had assumed as an expression of royal power and taste, and as a major setting for court life. In gardens of such scale, dominated by a central axis and extended vista, and with a wealth of statuary and lavish water displays, the role of topiary and shaped plants is integral but subordinate. The flowing lines of the embroidered parterres are traced in clipped boxwood. Topiary specimens, often combined with flowers, mark accents in the borders surrounding the parterres and, planted in containers, are used to line walks. Clipped hedges of *charmilles* (hornbeam), often trimmed to a considerable height, line the walks and the *bosquets*.

In the 17th and early 18th centuries Versailles became the ultimate standard of taste, not least in matters of garden design. The French Baroque garden was copied throughout Europe: at Drottningholm in Sweden, the Russian Peterhof on the Gulf of Finland and the imperial palace of Schönbrunn in Vienna, not to mention countless lesser courts in Europe. Embroidered parterres, topiary and hedges were inevitably part of what had become an international garden style. In the Netherlands, however, the French influence was blended with a native tradition of garden making that had developed with the emergence of the Dutch republic in the early 17th century. The rectilinear Dutch canal garden, of modest scale even at its most princely, fitted into the region's flat landscapes divided up by drainage canals. The arrangement of its compartments, parterres, hedged walks and orchards surrounded by trees and canals was essentially static.

The influence of French garden design is seen most strikingly in the ornamentation of the embroidered parterres and in the lavish waterworks of Het Loo. These gardens, now impressively restored, were created in 1688–89 by William of Orange after the Glorious Revolution, when he and his wife Mary became joint monarchs of Britain. Het Loo also shows strong Dutch characteristics, including geometric boxwood and yew topiary, and

OPPOSITE A modern style of gardening draws heavily on Dutch traditions but uses a wide range of flowering and foliage plants within a formal structure that is underlined by topiary, hedges and pleached or mopheaded trees. The style is particularly well suited to small and medium-size gardens on the flat that are screened from the world beyond by hedges and walls.

tunnel arbors, with trees trained onto a trellis framework.

The influence of Dutch gardens was felt strongly in Britain during the reign of William and Mary. Their most ambitious undertaking was at Hampton Court (where the Privy Garden has recently been restored). The Great Fountain Garden was an elaborately embroidered parterre of dwarf boxwood designed—like that at Het Loo—by the Huguenot Daniel Marot. As well as the numerous fountains, there was a prodigious quantity of topiary, including pyramids of yew and balls or domes of bay and holly. It is the use of clipped "greens" more than the delight in the flower garden that came to represent the characteristic feature of Dutch-influenced gardens in Britain—and, too, in the United States, as at Colonial Williamsburg in Virginia. However, the use of topiary to excess, and the tight and fussy order of the gardens it filled must have played a role in the movement of taste toward greater informality, as favored by writers such as Joseph Addison and Alexander Pope. Once fashion had dictated a change, the fate of the topiary garden in Britain was sealed. As the landscape garden gathered momentum, the scale of the destruction makes the survival of Levens Hall in Cumbria—an outstanding topiary garden that retains some of the original trees of the layout made between 1689 and 1712—all the more miraculous. It was not only in Britain that the landscape garden swept away those ordered layouts in which shaped and trained plants were an important component. Nevertheless, in Continental Europe topiary and formal gardens of hedged compartments maintained a much more secure hold than in Britain, where it was not until the Victorian period that they were rediscovered, with particular relish, by Arts and Crafts gardeners.

There is, however, another world of topiary, which seems to have been little influenced by fashionable trends in gardening. Giant birds looming over diminutive cottages; a railway engine, nearly life-size, parked beside a bungalow; a fox fleeing along a hedge top pursued by a pack of hounds—these and countless other expressions of the gardener's fantasy may be mysterious, amusing or charmingly whimsical, even when they lapse from conventional notions of good taste. Part of their appeal often lies in their random placing, as if topiarists have been suddenly overwhelmed by

irresistible inspiration. They are perhaps the true descendants of the "hunt scenes, fleets of ships and all sorts of images" in cypress described by Pliny the Elder in the 1st century A.D. Some would say that the highly personal crafting of whimsical shapes from living plants is the most vital thread in the long history of topiary and warrants being thought of as folk art. As well as being private and small scale, it is capable of monumental expression. One of the most sensational topiary gardens of the 20th century is the cemetery at Tulcan in Ecuador. There its creator, Don José Maria Azuel Franco, has clipped *Cupressus arizonica* into a formidable architectural complex, with geometric and representational topiary, which in its details harks back to the visual arts of pre-Columbian America. The adaptation of these details to topiary is a reminder of the countless decorative motifs from many cultures that can provide the inspiration for simple designs cut out of living plants. At Disneyland topiary takes another direction, more commercial art than folk art, with forms based on the powerful images of the television and movie screen.

Tools and equipment of the craft

The equipment used by gardeners remained little changed over centuries until the introduction of powered tools. Roman gardeners would have known single-handed shears (similar to those used for shearing sheep) and sickles but they probably did close trimming of tough growth with sharp knives. In the early 17th century there were already wooden-handled scissor-action shears very similar to those used today, and even relatively sophisticated versions of remote-control shears and pruners, but it was not until the 19th century that hand pruners challenged the pruning knife as the standard tool for detailed work.

Experienced operators of powered tools usually have no difficulty using fast-cutting equipment on topiary. However, most gardeners prefer using hand shears in the way gardeners have done for hundreds of years, working methodically to avoid removing too much growth at a time. Plants with relatively large leaves such as bay laurel (*Laurus nobilis*) that would look mutilated if trimmed with shears can be shaped with hand pruners. The trimming tools used for topiary are also suitable for trimming hedges. However,

A healthy and intriguing side of topiary, reflecting the fantasy and skill of individual gardeners, pays scant regard to ideas of good taste. This innocent alligator has been shaped out of fast-growing *Lonicera nitida*, which needs several trims annually to achieve the superb finish shown here. Hand shears are normally used for trimming detailed topiary but cordless electric hedgetrimmers are useful if there are many shapes to trim.

the renovation of an old hedge calls for additional equipment. A long-handled pruner is invaluable but you need a saw to cut through thick stems. Double-edged pruning saws, which have coarse teeth on one edge and fine teeth on the other, can be difficult to operate in a confined space. The Grecian saw, which has a curved blade and cuts only on the pull stroke, is more versatile.

The availability of powered hedgetrimmers has greatly reduced the labor involved in cutting a long hedge. The most useful powered hedgetrimmers have double- or reciprocating-action blades, usually 16–24in (40–60cm) long. Those powered by electricity have the great advantage of being relatively light. The use of a residual current device (RCD) protects the circuit but the trailing cable is a hazard and the equipment must be operated within 100ft (30m) of the power supply. Gasoline-powered hedgetrimmers are noisier and heavier but can be operated anywhere. There are also battery-operated hedgetrimmers, for which the source of power has to be moved about the garden. Cordless hedgetrimmers powered by a rechargeable battery are not up to cutting thick stems and in any case need recharging too

frequently to make them useful for trimming long stretches of hedge. However, of all the powered tools they are the most suitable for trimming small specimens of topiary. By being properly fitted with goggles, ear protectors and heavy-duty gloves, gardeners reduce the discomfort and risks of using powered tools.

A high proportion of the accidents associated with hedge trimming occur when gardeners are working above ground level. Lightweight aluminum ladders are easy to move about the garden, but a firm level platform is more secure and makes it possible to work much more efficiently. Wheeled platforms of various kinds were used in large formal gardens before the development of hydraulic cherry pickers, those for trimming tall lindens and hornbeams lining avenues being of considerable height. In a medium-size garden a combination of planks and folding trestles can make a firm platform and the materials can be stored in a relatively small space.

Useful equipment for laying out beds includes garden line, stakes and a tape measure. A rule, often handier to use than a tape measure, can be made from a straight length of wood 5–10ft

(1.5–3m) long and 2in (5cm) by ½in (1cm), marked at 4in (10cm) intervals. A spirit level and plumb line give accurate horizontals and verticals, although many gardeners manage to get their hedges straight and true without ever using them. Aids to precision useful when a topiary shape is repeated—as in an avenue—include a large-scale right angle in wood and large-scale dividers.

Templates and formers for particular shapes and batters (tapered hedge sides) may have to be specially made. A template made from an upright beam with an arm to indicate the slope, hinged from the bottom, can be adjusted to give different batters, the arm being held in the desired position at points along a horizontal crosspiece attached by pegs to the top of the upright. Formers made with a wooden frame and side panels made of wire mesh are relatively easy to construct for cubes and angled shapes; these can be set over plants, which are clipped to the shape as leaves grow through the wire panels. It is essential to get a former square and upright before trimming the plant. The ideal is to remove such a former once the shape is established; if left it tends to cause abrasion and to inhibit the development of the plant. It is usually necessary to dismantle the former and remove it piece by piece. Metal frames are used ornamentally, establishing well-defined geometric shapes some time before the topiary plants inside them are fully developed; these are generally treated as permanent.

Laying sheets of burlap or similar material before trimming begins makes cleaning up a less tiresome chore, enabling most of the clippings to be picked up quite easily. Even so, the tidy gardener needs a rake and broom.

Overcoming problems with topiary and hedges

Many of the numerous insects and countless microorganisms that populate a garden are either beneficial or harmless to plants. Pests, diseases and disorders that can damage, disfigure and kill are, however, the dark side of gardening. The gardener is in some cases the servant of troublemakers, generously bringing together, in a confined space, plant victims to suit particular tastes. Pests and diseases specific to a particular plant stand the best chance of flourishing where it grows in quantity, as in a hedge. Even so, serious problems are most often associated with poor growing conditions; struggling plants are less resistant to attack than those that are growing vigorously. Such potential problems may appall the novice, but it is reassuring that experienced gardeners tend to be phlegmatic about them.

Sound garden practice rather than extravagant use of chemicals is the best defence against pests, diseases and disorders. Good drainage is essential, as troublesome fungal diseases such as dieback and *Phytophthora* often affect plants that are growing in waterlogged conditions. The ground needs to be cleared of weeds and then dug thoroughly, well in advance of planting. Nutrient-rich and moisture-retaining organic matter can be added when the ground is dug. Planting, to some extent geared to local conditions, particularly climate, must be timed to give topiary and hedges the best chance of getting established quickly (see the Directory, page 148). Once the hedge is planted, mulches help to retain moisture but some watering may be necessary in extended dry spells. The base needs to be kept clear of weeds, most importantly ivy. When it comes to the annual application of a slow-release fertilizer in the garden, the hedge is often the forgotten feature, even though its close planting means that nutrients can be quickly exhausted.

In trying to identify problems of trees and shrubs grown as topiary and hedges, and to some extent the problems of climbers, it is helpful to know the broad categories of pests, diseases and disorders (information on specific plants is given in the Directory, page 148). There are three main groups of organisms that cause disease in plants. The symptoms of virus infections often show in stunted growth, distortion and yellow mottling of the leaves. Viruses are spread when sap from an infected plant is transferred to another plant by, for example, a sap-feeding pest or a pruning tool. The numerous fungal infections, spread from plant to plant by airborne or waterborne spores (usually just large enough to be visible to the naked eye), include leaf spots, mildews and rusts as well as those with more conspicuous structures, such as the bracket fungi. Several bacterial infections, including *Phytophthora*, are soil-borne; others may be transferred from one plant to another by insects. These often cause rapid deterioration of the plant at the site of the infection. In addition to these diseases there are a number of physiological disorders that often show in stunted

Where the common yew is not hardy enough to withstand severe winter conditions, *Taxus x media*, its hybrid with the hardier Japanese yew (*T. cuspidata*), first raised in the U.S.A. in 1900, is sometimes used as an alternative. It makes splendidly dense hedges that can be trimmed to a very sharp finish, as these superbly maintained examples show.

growth and discolored foliage. These have various, sometimes multiple causes, among them mineral deficiencies.

Some of the most troublesome plant pests are those that feed on sap, which they suck through a needle-like mouthpart that is inserted into the plant. They include adelgids, aphids, red spider mite and scale insects. Infestations may cause leaf distortions and the formation of galls (which can also be caused by bacteria and fungi). Some sap-feeding pests, particularly aphids, excrete sugary honeydew, which is prone to becoming infected with an unsightly sooty mold, a non-parasitic fungus. Sap-feeders are often responsible for transmitting viruses from an infected plant to others. In their larval stage many insects live underground, feeding on roots, and the damage they cause is often discovered only at a late stage. The effect of leaf-eating pests is more obvious. They include the caterpillars of butterflies and moths, and the adult forms of several insects, including the vine weevil. Larger pests that can cause considerable damage to leaves and stems include deer, mice, rabbits, squirrels and voles. Dogs can be exasperating:

their urine scorches foliage. And then there are children.

Chemical controls are usually fast-acting and are widely used to control pests and diseases. They must satisfy strict safety standards before they can be marketed; however, the mistakes of the past and concern for the environment have made many gardeners uneasy about using them. They are available in various forms, including contact sprays, which kill pests or fungal spores directly, and systemic sprays, which are absorbed into the plant and in this way kill, for example, sap-sucking insects. If you are using chemical sprays, you must follow the manufacturer's instructions closely and store any unused chemicals in a safe place. Avoid repeated use of the same pesticide or fungicide over a long period, as pests and fungi may develop tolerance. No chemical controls are effective against viruses. The range of chemicals is under constant review, so gardeners must check what is currently available to control specific pests and diseases. The much smaller range of products available to organic gardeners includes those such as derris that are made from "natural" ingredients.

PLANTS as SCULPTURE

A potted boxwood spiral and a foursome of low
mopheads shaped from *Lonicera nitida* form
the centerpiece of this herb garden.

Simple geometric shapes

Of all the shapes in the topiary repertoire, the most versatile are those of simple geometry. Topiary balls, cones, pyramids and obelisks, and to a lesser extent cubes and cylinders, were a mainstay of the great formal French and Dutch gardens of the 17th century; their ranked orders can still be seen in surviving or restored gardens such as those of Versailles and Het Loo. With adjustments of scale and number, such simple geometric topiary translates with astonishing ease to even the smallest modern town and country gardens. A single specimen can make a telling point; in the case of a container-grown specimen the pot or tub forms part of its geometry, a fact best appreciated when in the failing light of dusk plant and container fuse to make a single impression. A pair might mark a transition in the garden or frame a feature. More elaborate sequences can form avenues to underscore the axes of a garden. Even when they are used sparingly in a domestic setting, simple shapes convey something of the timeless serenity that distinguishes formal topiary gardens of monumental scale.

Suitable plants for simple shapes

Geometric topiary is mainly formed from specimens of densely bushy small-leaved evergreens of slow to moderate growth. The most favored plants in temperate regions are common boxwood and, for larger specimens, yew. In the past many other plants have been used, the Italian or Mediterranean cypress, for instance, which had supreme status in the magnificent architectural gardens

LEFT A combination of simple balls and more complicated shapes in boxwood are staged in a small-scale but dramatic arrangement, in conjunction with a pair of stone lions, one of which is shown here. Some of the topiary specimens are grown in beds while others are planted in white-painted terra-cotta pots.

OPPOSITE A graveled path leading from a brick-paved area shaded by a canopy of grapevines (*Vitis vinifera*) enters a garden compartment in which small beds are edged with dwarf boxwood. The centerpiece is a ball-topped square in boxwood. Simpler conical shapes are placed to underline the geometric layout of the beds; they are repeated on a larger scale in the compartment beyond, standing in mown grass, a sober contrast to a colorful summer border.

The entrance to a walled garden is flanked by terra-cotta urns with young
boxwood topiary trained as balls. Pleached lindens opposite give the garden
privacy. Inside the compartment, boxwood cones in terra-cotta pots are
combined with shaped boxwood growing in the open ground.

SHAPING A BOXWOOD BALL

These instructions are for shaping a container-grown specimen into a ball with a height of about 12in (30cm). A plant growing in the open garden can be shaped in a similar way. The technique for training a boxwood ball on a stem is in essence the same as for training a mophead bay (see page 32).

MATERIALS REQUIRED
A potted, untrimmed specimen of boxwood (*Buxus sempervirens*), about 18in (45cm) in height and circumference, making dense and even growth
Shears

A   B   C

1 In early summer, set the potted specimen on a bench or raised surface in a well-lit position.
2 Turn it around to assess how much growth you need to remove to form the basis of a neat ball with a circumference of about 12in (30cm).
3 Working freehand and making even movements, trim a horizontal band defining the circumference of the ball. Be careful not to make the first cuts too deep—you can always trim further if necessary. (A)

4 With the shears turned over, so that the angled blades curve over the plant, cut a band across the top, defining the upper curve of the ball. (B)
5 With the shears pointing down and turned back again so that the normal face of the blades is against the plant, cut away excess growth left between the upper and central bands.
6 Following the shape of the upper half, trim the lower half of the plant to soil level, so that the ball seems to be sitting on the soil. (C)

7 Run your hands over the shape to remove trimmings.
8 Now assess the trimmed shape, turning the specimen around and standing back to make sure that the ball is symmetrical. If adjustments are necessary, trim lightly and assess again. There may be gaps, especially in the upper part of the ball, until new growth fills these out.
9 Trim again between mid- and late summer and once or twice each subsequent summer.

---

of Renaissance Italy. Where bold mass is more important than clean lines, trees and shrubs with larger and coarser leaves, such as Portugal laurel (*Prunus lusitanica*) and species of holly (*Ilex*), are practical alternatives to plants with small dense foliage.

The disadvantage of fast-growing plants, in particular the privets (*Ligustrum*) and boxleaf honeysuckle (*Lonicera nitida*), is that they require several trims in the growing season if they are to hold their shape. They are generally dismissed as plants of second rank, although a neatly rounded specimen of the golden privet (*Ligustrum ovalifolium* 'Aureum') makes a spectacularly radiant globe. The relatively rare examples of deciduous topiary are domes or cubes of hawthorn (*Crataegus*), which make tight growth when regularly trimmed. Even in their leafless state they are graphically geometric.

The considerable variation in growth and color is an attractive feature of many plants used for topiary, particularly boxwood and yew. However, when choosing plants to make a matching pair or to form an avenue, where uniform growth and color are important, the best course is to use plants of the same clone, propagated from cuttings taken from the same parent.

Training simple shapes

Trained geometric topiary, particularly in boxwood, which does better in containers than yew, is widely available. The time and labor of training is inevitably reflected in the cost but a high initial outlay on a small number of plants may be justified to give a new garden a mature framework.

Even when gardeners train their own specimens it does not take too long to achieve a mature effect, provided the untrained plants used as the raw material are healthily vigorous and already well developed. The ideal is to start with a young specimen, a little

SHAPING A BOXWOOD CONE

These instructions are for shaping a container-grown specimen into a cone with a height of about 20in (50cm). A plant growing in the open garden can be shaped in a similar way, to whatever height is required, but the leader should not be cut until it is approximately 2in (5cm) above the desired height.

MATERIALS REQUIRED

A potted, untrimmed specimen of boxwood (*Buxus sempervirens*), about 24in (60cm) in height and circumference, making dense and even growth and having a strong central leader

Shears

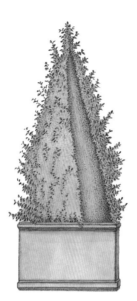
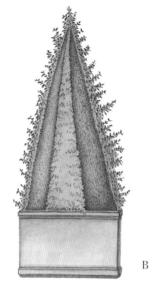

A   B   C

1 In early summer, place the potted specimen on level ground.
2 Standing over it, with your eye fixed on the central vertical line and holding the shears pointing downwards at the angle required for the shape of the cone, clip downwards from the centerpoint in a strip defining the edge of the cone. (A)
3 Repeat all the way around the plant. (B)
4 Remove trimmings.
5 Stand back and assess the cone. There may be gaps, but if the cone is kept well watered and fed, new growth will eventually fill these in. If further trimming is needed, work over the whole plant again.
6 Trim again between mid- and late summer.
7 In subsequent years, trim the cone once or twice each summer.

taller than the intended shape, which has been lightly trimmed for several years to encourage dense, even growth. You can then cut it down to the required height and shape, although it may take two or three years to achieve complete symmetry.

In the established garden it is worth maintaining a nursery of seedlings or cuttings, which after the first two years can have their laterals trimmed to make the plants bush out. However, gardeners starting from such beginnings must reconcile themselves to a wait of several years before they have material large enough to shape more specifically. It may take five years or more for boxwood cuttings, for instance, to become large enough to be shaped into cones 24in (60cm) high. If you are aiming for a really tall and substantial specimen, such as a yew cone 8ft (2.5m) or more high, the plant will need to grow in height as well as in bulk. It may take more than ten years to shape a vigorous yew plant 4–6ft (1.2–1.8m) high into a substantial cone over 8ft (2.5m) in height, cutting back the leader only when the required height has been reached.

Plants for geometric shapes must have well-balanced growth and for most it is best if this is growing evenly around a vigorous main stem or leader. Cuttings taken from side shoots do not produce strong leaders but make bushy horizontal growth, and are therefore suitable for low cubes and cylinders. To maintain balanced growth, the plants need an open position uncrowded by other plants and fertile, moist but well-drained soil. The application of an organic mulch and a slow-release chemical fertilizer in spring will encourage healthy growth. Well-developed container-grown specimens that are moved to the open garden or replanted in another container generally need about a year to become established: only then should you start shaping them.

Much training of topiary is done by eye. You need to establish a central vertical line, the key to creating a symmetrical shape, and when clipping constantly assess the shape from all sides to ensure that it remains balanced. Curved surfaces are generally easier to train than the angled geometry of cubes and pyramids. Where a shape is repeated, as in an avenue, aids to precision such as rules, templates and formers (see page 16) are almost indispensable.

ABOVE A number of dwarf boxwood plants set close together can be trimmed to form low, flat topiary shapes.

RIGHT The central leader of these bay laurels has been kept growing to form slender spires, but trimming of the lower branches has encouraged bushy growth at the base.

Maintaining simple shapes

Far from being a chore, the regular trimming regime necessary to maintain topiary shapes is often a source of great pleasure to hands-on gardeners. Some are happy only when the lines of their topiary are clean and sharp. This means trimming twice a year, in early and late summer, even relatively slow-growing boxwood and yew. However, a simple shape with its outline haloed by a fuzz of new growth has its own charm. You can enjoy the contrast between a phase of soft growth and the firmness that follows trimming by clipping boxwood and yew only once a year, which is sufficient to keep shapes in good order. A single trim is best given in late summer: trimming earlier results in excessive growth before winter; trimming later exposes plants to the risk of frost damage.

It is most effective to trim steadily and methodically, using the mature shape as a guide, and clipping each season's new foliage and shoots back to the old growth. Less rigorous pruning will result in an expanding shape that will eventually require drastic renovation. Very large topiary shapes inherited when taking over a garden may

In this garden formal components give continuity while rich planting
provides a changing display through the seasons. Only the most practiced
and confident gardener could ensure the geometric precision of the dense
boxwood pyramids without resorting to the use of a former.

USING A FORMER TO SHAPE A YEW OBELISK

*These instructions are for creating an obelisk 7ft (2.2m)
high. A former may be made of wood and mesh or of
metal. For best results it might be easier to have it
custom-made. You can use it during the initial
training and subsequently when you clip the shape.*

MATERIALS REQUIRED

A young, vigorous yew (*Taxus baccata*)
growing in the open garden, about 4½ft
(1.4m) high and having a strong central
leader. The plant should have been lightly
trimmed for two or three years to encourage
dense, even growth and it should be well
furnished with foliage to the ground

A former, consisting of a wooden frame
6½ft (2m) high, 40in (1m) square at the
base and 20in (50cm) square at the top,
with firm wire-mesh panels in the sides but
with the top and bottom open

Shears

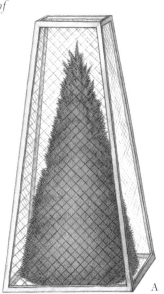
A

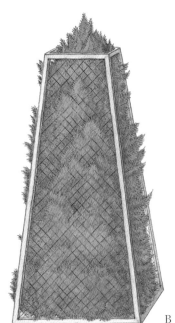
B

C

1 In early summer, begin shaping the yew by
clipping it into the shape of a symmetrical cone
in proportion to the dimensions of the former.
Do not cut the leader.
2 In late summer of the same year, trim again
lightly, still leaving the leader uncut, and then
set the former over the plant, ensuring that it is
centered on the plant and square. (A)

3 In early and late summer in subsequent years,
trim any shoots that grow through the mesh of
the former, but allow the leader to continue
growing, cutting it only when it has grown to
about 12in (30cm) above the former. (B)
4 Once the leader has been cut, when trimming
the sides in early and late summer clip the top
of the plant to a central point extending about

10in (25cm) above the former to create a
pyramid shape.
5 When the shape of the main body is
complete, with the plant filling out the
shape of the former, remove the former. (C)
6 Trim the obelisk once or twice annually
in summer, clipping back to the old growth,
preferably using the former as a guide.

seem daunting at first, but the technique for trimming these is
essentially the same as for smaller specimens.

The most versatile tool for clipping is a pair of sharp, well-oiled
hand shears, and shears are usually the best choice for small-leaved
plants such as boxwood and yew. It is best to set the base of the
blades as nearly as possible at the same angle as the surface being
cut, and move the handles together and apart evenly as the shears
work. For curved surfaces it may prove easier to work with the
shears turned over, the upper surface of the blades against the
foliage being cut. An initial snipping out of small cuts as guide
marks is helpful, particularly on large plants—usually from the
bottom up so that trimmed shoots are not caught up in the growth
being cut. Powered tools are laborsaving but operate at a speed

that can make an inadvertent slip seriously damaging. In
experienced hands a mechanical hedgetrimmer is useful for dealing
with large plants, the long blade being good for maintaining
large flat surfaces and right angles. Shears and hedgetrimmers
leave a surface of mutilated leaves, which can look unattractive
on large-leaved plants. Cutting off whole leaves or sprigs of foliage
with hand pruners results in a slightly looser shape but keeps
the leaves intact.

As well as needing regular trimming, to achieve their potential
topiary shapes must be kept weed-free at the base, fed annually
with a general slow-release fertilizer and well watered during
periods of drought. But the contribution they make to the garden
far exceeds the amount of work involved in looking after them.

Simple shapes on stems

You can extend the range of simple topiary shapes by training them on a leg or clear stem. Pruning to form standards—that is, shrubs or trees grown on a single stem from which the lower branches have been removed—is widely applied in gardens and in landscape planting. It lightens the effect of individual specimens or groups of trees such as avenues planted to give height, and simplifies the maintenance of lawns and underplanting. It is easy to shape the head of a plant that tolerates regular trimming to form a symmetrical sphere or dome. These balls on stems, sometimes refered to as "mopheads" or "lollipops," and dome or mushroom shapes are by far the most common of the simple shapes. Other shapes that are occasionally seen include cones, pyramids and cubes, the latter sometimes being organized in a sequence, like separated segments of a stilt hedge (see page 104).

Shapes on stems are particularly effective in the smaller garden, where there is a tendency for low planting that keeps the eye fixed at ground level. Hovering accents lift the eye, transforming the garden from a two-dimensional carpet to a three-dimensional space. They may be used as cornerpieces and centerpieces, arranged as sentry-like pairs flanking doors and benches, or planted more grandly as avenues. Planting them in containers, such as suitably formal Versailles tubs, gives extra height, which can be further extended by setting the container on a plinth. In container gardening a mophead or lollipop is effective as a sharply defined finial or finishing ornament to an exuberant flowery base.

Scale and proportions

The scale and proportions of shapes on stems vary considerably according to the plant grown. Boxwood, one of the shrubs commonly used for this purpose, is usually grown on a stem 12–24in (30–60cm) high, with the spherical head 6–12in (15–30cm) in diameter. The ever-popular bay laurel, an allusion to sunny Mediterranean gardens even when grown in cooler regions, can easily be trained on a stem 4–6ft (1.2–1.8m) high, with a head 18–24in (45–60cm) across. When trained as a substantial dome not less than 24in (60cm) across the base it looks altogether more serious. Hornbeam (*Carpinus betulus*), an exception among the plants mentioned here in being deciduous, may sometimes be seen trained with a stem clear to a height of about 8ft (2.5m), supporting a cube about 30in (75cm) in height. In conditions where it is hardy enough, the live oak (*Quercus virginiana*), which growing naturally is capable of making a massive tree, can be trained with a head 8–10ft (2.5–3m) across on a clear stem 10–12ft (3–3.7m) in height. Although an avenue of specimens on this scale is an impressive sight, you should be aware before planting that its long-term maintenance entails work from ladders and trestles.

The range of shrubs and trees commonly trained to carry simple geometric shapes on clear stems is, in fact, quite small. The most popular of those not already mentioned are myrtle (*Myrtus*), which is usually trained on a stem 12–30in (30–75cm) high, and taller plants such as the common juniper (*Juniperus communis*), hollies, Portugal laurel and yew. However, adventurous gardeners may experiment with a wide range of other trees and shrubs, among them several conifers. Even the much vilified Leyland cypress (x *Cupressocyparis leylandii*) quickly makes a stout stem on which can be shaped an attractive loose head of foliage—yellow and feathery in the case of the cultivar 'Castlewellan'; *Cupressus arizonica* var. *glabra*, with blue-gray foliage, and *C. macrocarpa*, especially the cultivar 'Goldcrest,' with rich yellow foliage, are other conifers to try. There is plenty of scope, too, for experimenting with broad-leaved evergreens. The smaller the leaf the denser the head, but even large-leaved plants, such as *Elaeagnus angustifolia* and species of *Pittosporum*, are capable of forming dense heads comparable to those of the bay laurel. It is important to choose plants that are hardy enough for the conditions in which they are to be grown.

OPPOSITE Paired standards are often part of a hierarchy of shapes that lift the eye to a gate, door or eye-catcher. In this garden mopheads of bay laurel are preceded by a pair of boxwood balls, but the stone *fleur de lis* that the standards flank is so low that it catches the eye for only a moment; the viewer's attention is prepared by the trimmed heads to move from the ordered garden to the wilder planting beyond the hedges. The leaves of the bay laurel, which are formed in tight clusters, remain whole, as the result of using hand pruners for pruning.

LEFT The planting of two types of standards establishes the rhythmic formality of this narrow garden compartment. Garden seats are set out between evenly spaced tall standards of the mophead acacia (*Robinia pseudoacacia* 'Umbraculifera'). Facing each seat is a container-grown mopheaded standard of the evergreen oak, the containers set inside large baskets.

OPPOSITE LEFT The Kilmarnock willow (*Salix caprea* 'Kilmarnock'), a compact male form of the goat willow, is rarely more than 6½ft (2m) high and has a naturally dense head of stiffly weeping branches. Light trimming forms a regular dome.

OPPOSITE RIGHT Stout-stemmed standards of *Myrtus communis* subsp. *tarentina* have been tucked into the corners of boxwood-edged beds on each side of a garden path.

Initial training of standards

The method of training for a mophead bay laurel (see page 32) can be adapted to different trees and shrubs. The essential aim is the development of a strong stem, which is cut back at a height of approximately the centerpoint of the projected head. A specimen with uneven lower growth, therefore unsuitable for training as a solid shape, is fine for training as a standard. Mopheads to be grown as pairs should be matched for size and robustness.

A common fault of standards is that the stems are weak. This may happen because some plants never quite establish themselves or because the lower side shoots, important for the development of a strong stem, have been removed prematurely. Although they can be shortened, you must not take them off until the main stem is sturdy enough to support itself. Many standards will need a stake or cane for support, which helps to straighten out kinks. The most pleasing are those that when mature need no support at all.

Maintenance of standards

The clipping regimes and general maintenance of standards follow that of other simple shapes (see page 25). It is best to trim all the larger-leaved plants, including bay laurel and Portugal laurel, with hand pruners rather than shears so that the surface of the shape is not composed of mutilated leaves. Remove suckers produced on the stem below the head or from ground level as soon as they appear. The standard comes into its own when the head seems to float above looser planting below it, but in that case it faces competition from other plants for nutrients and water, for which the gardener has to compensate, particularly when the plant is in the confined space of a container. As rainwater does not always penetrate the compost in pots and tubs, running off the foliage outside rather than inside the container, watering is often necessary in wet as well as in dry weather.

Even standards of plants that are otherwise relatively hardy,

TRAINING A MOPHEAD OF BAY LAUREL

The following instructions are for shaping a spherical head on a bay laurel stem 5ft (1.5m) high (from the top of the container to the midpoint of the head). Whatever the size of the head being trained, it is important to aim for a well-proportioned specimen. A pleasing ratio, although many variations are possible, is the diameter of the head approximately one-third the height of the stem below. The method for training a dome- or mushroom-shaped head on a single stem, for which bay laurel is eminently suitable, is the same, except that the head is trimmed straight across the bottom.

MATERIALS REQUIRED

A bay laurel (*Laurus nobilis*) with a strong and straight leader 6½–8ft (2–2.5m) high (in the case of a pot-grown specimen, the height includes the container)

Hand pruners (trimming with shears will produce a tighter, more regular head but the leaves will be mutilated)

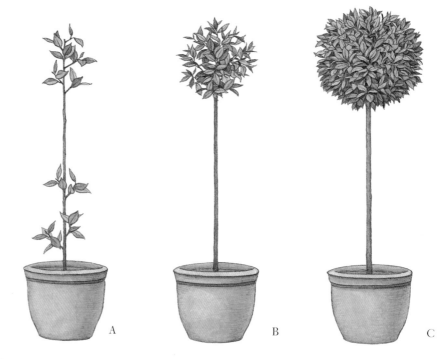

1 In early summer, cut back the leader just above a shoot about 6½ft (2m) from ground level.
2 At the same time, below the base of the projected head cut back several shoots to the main stem; but leave lower shoots, shortening them if they are lanky, to aid the development of a strong main stem.
3 Complete the initial training by trimming the shoots that will form the head, cutting them back to about 6in (15cm), just above a leaf. (A)

4 In late summer of the same year, trim the head again to the same length.
5 In early summer of the following year, trim the head to a roughly spherical shape and, if the stem is already providing a stout support, remove the lower branches completely. (B)
6 In late summer of the same year, trim the head again, working toward a spherical shape and, if the lower branches have not already been removed, cut them back to the main stem.

7 In subsequent years, trim the bay laurel head to make a sphere in early and late summer. (C) To maintain a balanced shapes first trim a horizontal band around the circumference to the required depth and then trim a central band over the top, using these bands as guides for shaping the rest of the head (see page 23). Remove any suckers that develop on the main stem or from ground level as soon as they appear.

whether in containers or in the ground, are vulnerable to frost damage. Where the winters are not too severe, insulation material around the stem, such as straw wrapped in burlap, will provide some protection. Sinking pot-grown plants in the ground so that the container is completely covered or wrapping the container in bubble wrap or other insulating material will help protect the roots from freezing. Where there is a serious risk of frost damage, move plants under cover during the coldest months.

Tropical and subtropical plants such as *Ficus benjamina* var. *nuda*, a form of the weeping fig that can be grown as a short standard with a small neat head, need special care. Some of these will be kept in a heated greenhouse all year round. Others that are hardier might be moved outdoors in summer, but as the days get cooler they will need protection, even if it is only provided by a conservatory. Hardier plants can be moved to an unheated glassed-in porch.

Variations on straight stems

You can give an otherwise simple standard a baroque flourish by training the stem in a spiral. This trick of gardening is relatively simple, provided the training is done while the stem is still young and flexible. It is most commonly practiced on bay laurel. For a whippy stem 3–4ft (90–120cm) high you have to start the training even before the head is formed. Wind a young leader around a vertical support in mid- to late summer, before the new green growth becomes woody. Avoid forcing, as this may cause the stem to split, but you can achieve a tight spiral by turning the leader around a single thick stake.

By substituting a cluster of three or four evenly spaced canes for the single stake it is possible to form a more generous spiral. It is a common mistake to remove the lower growths completely when winding the stem around its support. Some shortening is in order but, as with a straight stem, it is important to retain these shoots until the stem has thickened. Start training the head when the spiral is tall enough and remove the supporting stake when the stem is really sturdy.

Some virtuosic stunts rely on grafting techniques. In one of these the trunk divides and then joins up again; in another a lattice-work panel interrupts the main stem. Another eye-catching trick is to plait stems together. This is sometimes done with the tropical *Ficus benjamina*: single stems of three or four specimens are used and the roots of the different plants are trained out from the center so that the plants are not competing directly with one another for nutrients and moisture. Trained and grafted stems can even be shaped to form Chinese characters.

The sheltered zone of this paved terrace has been created with a highly successful planting of evergreens, in which subtle harmonies are based on a restricted palette and variations of shape and texture. Strong evidence of shaping, as in the boxwood topiary and the twisted stems of the bay laurel standards, is offset by the freer growth of plants such as ivies and cherry laurel. The numerous movable elements make it possible to restage the terrace in many different ways.

Flowering and fruiting standards

A large number of flowering and fruiting plants are grown as standards but to ensure a full display they are less tightly trimmed than topiary. Whether grown for ornamental or practical purposes, they are trained by one of two principal methods. The simplest of these for the amateur gardener involves training a main stem vertically, encouraging the development of a well-shaped head by cutting back the growing tip, and removing the lower leaves and side shoots to make a clean stem. With some plants, this technique does not produce a really sturdy stem and where this is the case —and also generally to simplify propagation and training in commercial nurseries—standards of these are formed by budding or grafting selected cultivars of a plant on the vertically trained stem of a rootstock. Whatever the technique used to form them, some pruning is generally necessary to maintain a balanced head, but close clipping of the kind used to shape geometric topiary would remove most of the flower buds that make these standards so ornamental and useful.

Flowering and fruiting standards need good growing conditions and a reasonably sheltered position. Even as mature specimens, almost all need supports, to which they can be attached by adjustable ties. Because a support takes away from a standard's ornamental value, it is tempting to use something light and inconspicuous, but a lame plant on an inadequate cane is sadder than an upright plant with a sturdy stake. A support should reach to just below the head of the plant. On an established plant two ties are generally sufficient, one just below the top of the stake and the other about one-third the height of the stake. Ties need to be checked regularly and loosened if they have become tight. Where

LEFT Rose standards are propagated by budding a cultivar on the stem of a suitable rootstock (usually in a nursery). Ideally the head of flowers should seem to float, almost as though it has no support, although the necessary staking often detracts from this impression.

OPPOSITE Herbaceous plants and mopheads of *Lonicera nitida* form an understory beneath lightly shaped domes of a splendid hawthorn, *Crataegus x lavalleei* 'Carrierei.'

ABOVE The common honeysuckle (*Lonicera periclymenum*) grown as a standard makes a fragrant centerpiece here, surrounded by lavender in a boxwood-edged compartment. As honeysuckle flowers on wood produced the previous season it should be shaped as soon as flowering has finished.

OPPOSITE Wisterias are surprisingly versatile vigorous climbers. By regular pruning they can be maintained as bushes or as standards. The best way of growing a wisteria on a short arbor is as a slightly extended standard. A two-phase pruning regime that checks vegetative growth in summer and reduces shoots to short spurs in winter promotes flowering. It is essential to control the size of the head.

a standard is grown for its practical value, as in the case of a fruit bush in the kitchen garden, the most effective way of supporting it is with a pair of stakes, one on either side of the stem.

Whether grown in containers or in the open garden, flowering and fruiting standards are often combined with underplanting. As with topiary standards, there is inevitably competition for nutrients and water when other plants grow close to the base of standards, which you will have to counteract by feeding and watering. Take special care when working the soil around standards to avoid damaging roots. Damage to standards grafted or budded on rootstocks may stimulate the development of suckers, which are likely to become dominant unless removed.

Standards trained on their own stems

An extensive range of flowering and fruiting plants, and a few that have decorative foliage, such as coleus (*Solenostemon*), can be trained as standards on their own stems. Among the most popular are shrubs and sub-shrubs with a long flowering season. Some of these, such as the numerous cultivars of *Hydrangea macrophylla*, are reasonably hardy. Many others that are popular in temperate gardens, among them the Paris daisy (*Argyranthemum frutescens*), fuchsias, heliotrope (*Heliotropium arborescens*) and pelargoniums, are more tender, requiring frost protection from autumn to spring. Outside the tropics and subtropics plants grown as standards belonging to these climatic zones, such as the fragrant *Gardenia augusta*, usually need greenhouse or conservatory conditions.

For centuries members of the citrus family have had a special status in temperate regions, being grown in containers under glass from fall to spring and, where the weather in summer is mild enough, being moved outdoors for several months. They are highly ornamental, especially when grown as standards, the inconspicuous but deliciously scented flowers followed by long-lasting fruits, slowly ripening to cheerful yellow or orange, that nestle among glossy dark green leaves. Most commercially propagated citrus fruits are grafted but you can easily grow many, including lemons (*Citrus limon*), from seeds. The seedlings, like small-fruited kumquat (*Fortunella japonica* and *F. margarita*) and the calamondin (× *Citrofortunella microcarpa*), can be trained on a single stem.

You can even train some climbers as standards. The early Dutch honeysuckle (*Lonicera periclymenum* 'Belgica') makes a sweetly fragrant mophead; you can train the stem, strongly staked, up to about 4½ft (1.4m). Standards of wisterias, among the most vigorous climbers of temperate gardens, usually have stems 5–6ft (1.5–1.8m) high. One way to get a straight stem is to cut back a young plant and train up a vigorous shoot in a plastic pipe about 2in (5cm) in diameter, which can be slipped off once the stem has reached the top. When the grape vine (*Vitis vinifera*), a fruiting climber of great vigor, is trained as a standard, with annual pruning maintaining a head of fruiting spurs, a relatively compact plant can produce a surprising amount of fruit. In a warm climate, and even in a conservatory, the numerous cultivars of bougainvillea are vivid climbers to train as standards and the papery bracts surrounding the flowers give a display that lasts for months.

The method of training a fuchsia standard (see page 38) can be adapted to the training of many other plants. Rates of growth will vary and on woody plants you will have to prune with hand pruners. As with all standards, it is important to develop a really sturdy stem. Leaves and even shortened laterals growing on the stem will help it to thicken up; if necessary, delay their removal until the head is well formed.

TRAINING A FUCHSIA STANDARD

Fuchsias trained as standards are kept growing through the winter. Where there is any risk of frost they need to be kept in a well-lit position under glass at a minimum temperature of 50°F (10°C). It takes about eighteen months to train a full standard, which has a stem height of 30–40in (75–100cm). A half-standard, with a stem height of 18–30in (45–75cm), takes about a year. Quarter-standards, with stems 10–18in (25–45cm) high, and miniature standards, less than 10in (25cm) high, can be trained in about six months. As their roots develop, plants need repotting into slightly larger containers, with longer canes being inserted when required. A full standard will ultimately need a 12in (30cm) pot.

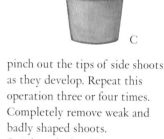

MATERIALS REQUIRED

A rooted cutting of a strong-growing fuchsia, taken in late summer, with leaves growing in sets of three (some fuchsias have leaves growing in sets of two)

A cane 10–20in (25–50cm) in height, and taller canes up to 55in (1.4m) high for full standards, to be used when potting; twist ties

No pruning tools are generally required, the growth being soft enough to pinch out between finger and thumb

1 In autumn, plant the cutting individually in a 4in (10cm) pot, at the same time inserting a cane close to the plant.
2 As the stem of the young plant lengthens, secure it to the cane with ties at intervals of about 3–4in (8–10cm). At this stage do not remove the lower leaves but once the stem is about 8in (20cm) high pinch out any side shoots that develop in the leaf axils. (A)

3 Six to eight weeks later, when the roots have filled the initial container, repot, inserting a longer cane if needed. Continue to train up the stem, removing side shoots but retaining leaves along the length of the stem.
4 When the plant has made three sets of leaves above the required height, pinch back the tip. (B)
5 To encourage the development of a well-balanced bushy head,

pinch out the tips of side shoots as they develop. Repeat this operation three or four times. Completely remove weak and badly shaped shoots.
6 When the head has started to fill out and the stem thickened, remove the lower leaves from the stem. Secure the standard to its support with ties, one just below the head and the other about one-third the way up the stem. (C)

Standards formed by budding and grafting

The initial training of standards formed by budding and grafting onto the stem of a rootstock usually takes place in the nursery. Standard roses are almost invariably trained in this way. The most elegant and best-proportioned of these, often listed as weeping standards, are formed by budding roses with flexible growth on stems 4½–6½ft (1.4–2m) high. Favorites for this treatment are Wichurana Ramblers, such as *Rosa* 'Albéric Barbier' and 'Minnehaha,' which flower once annually, in mid-summer. When these roses are in full flower, their stems, trailing almost to ground level, seem to be weighed down by their beautiful burden. A fully

grown specimen offers considerable wind resistance and therefore needs a stout stake. The flexible stems are sometimes tied into an umbrella-shaped wire framework fixed below the head. This makes the shape more regular and ensures that the stems hang down, but specimens with the stems draping naturally are more graceful. These Ramblers, which flower most freely on growths made the previous year, are maintained with a simple annual pruning regime in which a proportion at least of the old stems are cut out when flowering has finished. Trailing growth is also a feature of several Shrub roses that have a spreading habit, usually marketed as "ground cover" roses, which are sometimes available as standards. 'Nozomi,'

Fuchsias are readily trained as standards, and in this form they show off their dangling flowers well. In this garden matching single fuchsias planted in terra-cotta pots with a generous fringe of pelargoniums at their base make a combination that is bright with flowers over a long season. These fuchsias, which have been long-lived, are moved under glass annually as soon as there is a risk of frost in the fall.

which produces cascades of pearly pink flowers, is an attractive example. These roses require only light annual pruning between fall and spring.

Bush roses (still commonly known as Hybrid Teas and Floribundas), Shrub roses and Miniatures produce heads that vary considerably in size, but they are generally composed of more or less stiff and upright stems. These standards make up for their winter gauntness by flowering profusely in summer, in most cases repeating. They are a particular asset when combined with underplanting, establishing a formal tone and also creating layers of color in the garden.

The most attractive rose standards have lax stems, the cultivar being budded high enough on the rootstock to trail elegantly, sometimes to near ground level. In this kitchen garden, standards of a ground cover rose flanking a handsome container help to ensure that this part of the garden is not purely utilitarian. In the background on the left, sweet peas have needed little training to scramble up a support of hazel sticks. In the foreground are single-tier apple espaliers.

A full standard has a clear stem to a height of about 40in (1m). Shorter are half-standards, with stems about 30in (75cm) high, and quarter-standards, with stems only about 18in (45cm) high. Maintain standards of repeat-flowering roses by annual pruning between fall and mid-spring. Some may also need cutting back in autumn to reduce the risk of wind damage. The aim should be to remove any dead, diseased and damaged wood, and to maintain a balanced head. With Bush roses, you should cut back one or two of the oldest main stems to the union with the rootstock stem and other main stems by about half to outward-facing buds. It is better to prune Miniatures and repeat-flowering Shrub roses more lightly, cutting them back by about a third. Shrub roses that flower only once, such as *Rosa xanthina* 'Canary Bird,' are often the most difficult to maintain as balanced shapes. These roses benefit from having some old wood removed after flowering, and usually need additional thinning and light pruning between fall and mid-spring.

The most common traditional method of training many fruit trees is as standards, and in some cases their compact shapes are highly decorative. As different rootstocks for a particular plant are suited to different growing conditions, and also influence the way the plant grows, nurseries raise rootstocks in bulk and propagate selected cultivars by grafting or budding, which, as well as making commercial sense for the nurseries, has the advantage of making a wide choice of fruit tree rootstocks available for gardeners. There is a good range of rootstocks for apples, extending from the very dwarfing to the vigorous.

A particularly attractive fruit standard for the kitchen garden is the gooseberry, a soft bush fruit for cool conditions. (Check with your local office of the U.S. Department of Agriculture to see if gooseberries can be grown legally in your area.) Training up the naturally thorny shrub as a standard with an open-centered head, the fruiting spurs growing from six to eight permanent arms, helps to make fruit picking easier. You can train gooseberries to form standards on their own stems, as you can red and white currants, which have a similar pattern of growth. However, because the stems of gooseberries that are trained tend to be weak, standard goose-berries raised by commercial nurseries are normally grafted onto vigorous rootstocks of *Ribes divaricatum* or *R. odoratum*.

Susceptibility to American gooseberry mildew has counted against the gooseberry in the United States, but in Europe it is a popular bush fruit, and in the 19th century, its heyday as a show fruit, several hundred cultivars were available. Plants trained as standards are particularly ornamental when carrying fruit, whose color range includes greenish white, yellow, apple green and many shades of red and purple.

Topiary in an intimate garden

Front gardens are perfect for the bold and formal statement made by a geometrical design consisting almost entirely of topiary.

The garden is screened from the street by a yew hedge and a partly overlapping stilt hedge of hornbeam. There is a beautifully shaped arched gap above the gate, but the enclosed space seems strongly protected and secluded. The house itself forms one boundary and down the sides are walls extended by trellis. The level area, approximately 30ft (9m) square, is laid out symmetrically on each side of the central path, which is defined by a brick edging and a diamond pattern in a surface that is otherwise plain gravel. Halfway down the garden the path cuts through a raised bed, which has been planted to make a bold slash of a single color. Pink-flowered petunias have been used for a long-lasting summer display but other bright bedding would be just as effective, following on from winter and spring bedding of bulbs, polyanthus or winter-flowering pansies. Inside the raised beds, facing each other from each side of the garden, are columns of yew topped by balls—topiary alternatives to statuary.

Mophead standard hollies planted in four sets of three on the diagonal lift the eye. *Ilex aquifolium* 'Handsworth New Silver' has a crisp variegation; this female holly will fruit freely if there is a male clone near by. The middle of each set could be planted with a male clone such as *I. a.* 'Silver Queen' or a plain-leaved male holly. Each standard rises out of a square of lustrous curly-leaved ivy, *Hedera helix* 'Ivalace.' Pairs of yews, trimmed as interrupted columns, stand at each end of the path and pairs of blue-painted trellis obelisks, used simply as architectural shapes—although they could support climbing roses—flank the raised beds. Straight-rowed hedges and balls of boxwood under the windows make a neat finish.

This prelude to the house could be magically transformed at night by lighting the standards from below.

LEFT Hollies include some of the best broad-leaved evergreens for hedging, topiary shapes and standards. The berry crop is much reduced by clipping, but the foliage has year-round appeal. There are numerous cultivars of *Ilex × altaclerensis* and *I. aquifolium*; the plain-leaved kinds are lustrous deep green and the variegated hollies brightened by cream or silvery markings on green.

N

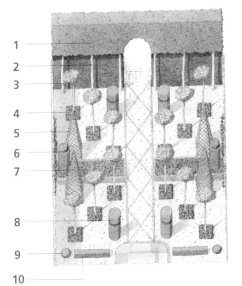

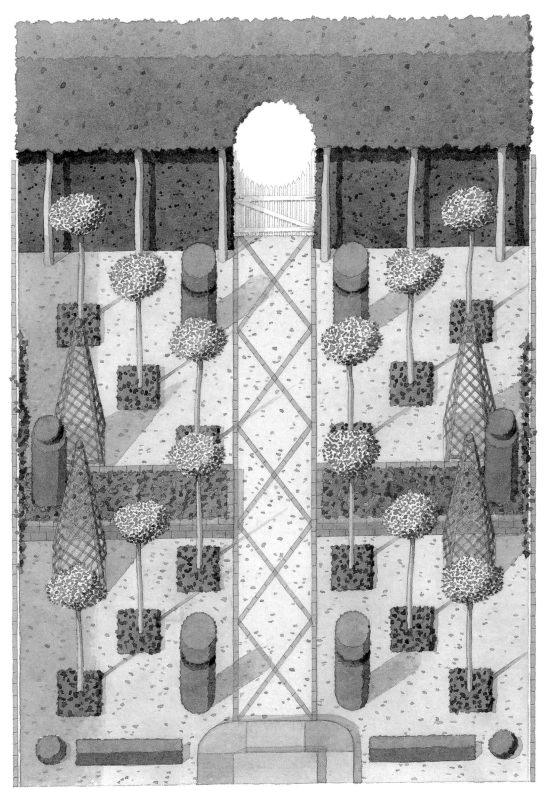

1 Stilt hornbeam hedge

2 Yew hedge

3 1 of 12 standards of variegated holly (*Ilex aquifolium* 'Handsworth New Silver')

4 1 of 12 squares of ivy (*Hedera helix* 'Ivalace')

5 1 of 4 trellis pyramids

6 1 of 2 ball-topped yew columns

7 1 of 2 beds seasonally planted with dwarf pink petunias

8 1 of 4 interrupted columns of yew

9 1 of 2 balls of dwarf boxwood

10 1 of 2 hedges of dwarf boxwood

Approximately 30ft (9m) square

Composite geometric shapes

You can greatly extend the topiary repertoire with various combinations of geometric shapes. The most common and most useful kind of block building consists of using one shape as a base or pedestal for another, in imitation of architectural or sculptural forms. Tiered arrangements and spirals may seem frivolous, but there is value in their relative lightness and sense of movement when set against the solid virtues of plainer geometric shapes.

Block building

Cones and pyramids sitting on cubes or cylinders and many other well-proportioned combinations convey a sense of calm solidity with more sophistication than the simple shapes themselves. Even when topiary is on the small scale of a boxwood specimen 30in (75cm) or less in height, a pedestal helps to give it distinction. On a grand scale, a change in shape interrupts bland and daunting surfaces and refines the sheer mass of clipped greenery. Combinations of more than two shapes can look contrived unless there is an architectural precedent for them, as for a cone or pyramid on a ball supported by a cube. There are good aesthetic reasons for the base being broader than the shape it is supporting. There is a good gardening reason, too, for shading of one shape by another, as a whole or a part, results in thin growth.

A composite geometric shape is usually formed from a single plant, which is lightly trimmed in the early stages to encourage dense growth and the development of a regular shape. You can usually start trimming the base before the plant has reached the desired height, though at this stage you should trim the growth above the base only on the sides. To give an appearance of solidity the base or pedestal must sit upright and level, and it is difficult to achieve precision without using rule, line and spirit level. After the initial shaping of the base there will probably still be gaps but these will fill in as the plant develops. You can start developing the second shape before the base is complete. The aim must be to get the shape centered on its base and vertical; this will again require the use of rule, line and spirit level. The difficulty of achieving geometric perfection is one reason why complex shapes are sometimes defined by metal frames; the frame also gives the complete outline even before the topiary it contains has reached

maturity. Frames are, however, a mixed blessing. They are often intrusive and may constrict or abrade growth of the fully developed plant. The mature shape of a specimen without a frame provides its own guide for trimming leaves and shoots back to the old growth. If you are planning a large-scale topiary you should give some thought to the way it will be maintained. Even a specimen about 5ft (1.5m) high may have to be trimmed from a ladder or a trestle if the base is broad.

Very large shapes that are broad at the base may be composed of more than one plant. Make sure that they are all of the same clone if you do not want differences in growth rate, leaf size and color to undermine the impression of a single architectural entity. On the other hand, interesting variation can be achieved intentionally by using two different plants to create a composite shape, one for the base and another for the shape above it. You could plant several golden yews (such as *Taxus baccata* 'Elegantissima') of the same clone around the base of a plain-leaved form of yew and shape them to form a yellow collar at the base of a dark green column. Or you might use boxwood as a square pedestal for a yew cone. Adding a base to an existing specimen is worth considering if you have inherited a large but undistinguished piece of topiary.

Tiered geometric shapes

There is a long history of training topiary with the shoots and foliage cut to form tiers, and these composite shapes have an enduring appeal. They are usually cut from fine-textured plants, particularly boxwood and yew, but larger-leaved plants, especially various hollies, although they produce a coarser effect, make very handsome specimens. The plant, of whatever kind, must have a strong and vertical central leader to support the tiers, which usually consist of a series of disks, each diminishing in thickness

OPPOSITE Stepped squares of boxwood with domed centers are arranged as two sets of four on each side of the main axis to a door. Low but large shapes such as these are created by planting several young specimens close together and then trimming the shape as though a single plant. The effectiveness of this geometric scheme depends on maintaining the levels throughout.

A variation on the tiered cakestand is topiary trained as a string of balls, here executed in yew. In the long term the regular growth of this shape is likely to be distorted by crowding on one side.

and diameter from bottom to top. The simplest kind of tiered arrangement consists of a finial standing clear but supported by the main stem above a larger shape. A "cakestand" in yew is typical of more complex arrangements. The specimen usually stands 8–10ft (2.5–3m) high and is composed of a pedestal, giving solidity and weight, and three to five tiers, each about 10–12in (25–30cm) thick and the same distance apart, topped by a ball or other finial. Topiary shapes with more numerous tiers look fussy and, if the gaps between the tiers are narrow, shading of one tier by another results in thin growth. The underside of a tier usually has sparse or little foliage because of shading.

In the initial stages of training a yew seedling to make such a shape, annual light trimming in summer encourages the development of a conical shape, well furnished with dense growth. The training of the tiers is commonly left until the yew is about 6½ft (2m) tall. You can save time by starting with a specimen close to this in height, but it should be well established in the growing position for at least a year before you start training the tiers. Even with a specimen of this size, it will take six to ten years to establish a mature plant with fully developed pedestal, tiers and finial. Although the aim is to create a balanced shape, it is often possible to make a tiered specimen from a plant that has gappy, irregular growth, provided the gaps occur in the spaces between the projected tiers.

To form the pedestal and tiers, cut growth back at intervals to leave sections of the main stem exposed. It is tempting to remove all branches and shoots in a band around the main stem that corresponds in depth to the intended gap. However, the shoots and foliage that will constitute a tier are often supported by branches springing from lower down on the main stem. It is essential to trace branches from the main stem to their extremities in order to establish, before making final cuts, whether the growth is dispensable. You can achieve much of the shaping to produce horizontal tiers by trimming, but you may need to pull branches down into position, using tarred string attached to the main stem or to branches in the level below. Ties are usually not needed for longer than a year but in any event you should check them from time to time and loosen them if they are constricting growth.

TRAINING A YEW CAKESTAND

A

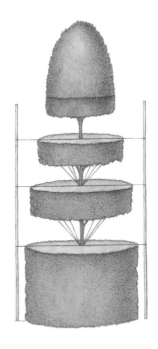

B

C

D

These instructions are for training a well-proportioned specimen about 9ft (2.7m) high; pedestal 30in (75cm) high, 4ft (1.2m) in diameter; first tier 12in (30cm) above the pedestal, 12in (30cm) thick, 40in (1m) in diameter; second tier 10in (25cm) above the first tier, 10in (25cm) thick, 32in (80cm) in diameter; third tier 10in (25cm) above the second tier, 8in (20cm) thick, 28in (70cm) in diameter; hemispherical finial 8in (20cm) above the third tier, 10in (25cm) high. However, there is scope for variation in the dimensions.

MATERIALS REQUIRED

A vigorous yew tree (*Taxus baccata*) with a straight leader approximately 6½ft (2m) high that has been established in the garden for at least a year and has been lightly trimmed to a conical shape

Garden line; level; tarred string

Shears; hand and long-handled pruners

1 In the summer of the first year, begin the development of the pedestal and the first and second tiers. Above the projected height of the pedestal, cut back branches to leave the main stem bare for about 10in (25cm). Above the projected first and second tiers, cut back branches to leave the main stem bare for about 8in (20cm).

The gaps between tiers will be greater than the cut lengths of bare stem because each tier is partly formed from growths that develop from below it on the stem.

2 At the same time, attach a length of garden line to the main stem and, pulling it out horizontally all the way around the plant as a guide for the radius (22in/55cm), trim the sides of the pedestal. (A)

3 Using tarred string attached to the main stem or lower branches, tie down upward-growing branches to a horizontal position. (B)

4 Again using string attached to the main stem as a guide to the radius (22in/55cm for the first tier, 16in/40cm for the second), trim the edges of the tiers.

5 Using garden line stretched between stakes as a horizontal guide, trim the upper surface of the pedestal and the first and second tiers so that they are level. Do not cut the leader, which must be allowed to develop to form the third tier and finial. (C)

6 In the summer of the next and subsequent years, trim the sides of the first two tiers to the required radius and cut the surface of the tiers level.

7 Also in the summer of the next or subsequent years, when the plant has made approximately another 16in (40cm) of growth, expose about 6in (15cm) of the main stem above the projected third tier. Tie down upward-growing branches of the third tier to a horizontal position.

8 Trim the third tier as in step 5.

9 When, as the wood ages, the stems of the tiers hold their position, remove the ties.

10 When the leader has grown about 2in (5cm) above the desired height, cut it back and trim as a half-sphere to make the finial. (D)

When clipping it is important to ensure that the pedestal and tiers are centered on the main stem. A simple way of checking is to use a garden line tied loosely to the main stem so that you can swing it around horizontally in a full circle. You can then use a knot tied at the appropriate radius as a measure, and make cuts with hand pruners to provide a guide for trimming the edge with shears. Use a line stretched between stakes and checked against a spirit level as a guide for trimming the horizontal surface of pedestal and tiers. Once the specimen is mature, it is usually not necessary to use guides, as trimming consists of cutting back to the old growth. Faultless vertical and horizontal lines and impeccable symmetry are the hallmarks of a well-trained cakestand but, it must be admitted, there is a quaint charm to specimens that have become wayward with age and their eccentric tilting is best preserved by trimming with indulgent sensitivity.

Another tiered arrangement, easier to shape by eye, consists of balls of foliage on a clear stem. The pedestal itself is often in the form of a large sphere, with a succession of balls above it, diminishing in size to the smallest, the finial. Boxwood, yew and hollies are much used for this kind of topiary. As when creating a specimen with disk-like tiers, it is essential to start off with a vigorous plant that has a straight and sturdy stem. The formative pruning consists of cutting growths back to the main stem to create gaps and then trimming, more severely than with disk-like tiers, to encourage the development of densely leafy balls. As with all tiered arrangements, you should not sever the leader until it has exceeded the desired height. You can then cut it back 2–4in (5–10cm) to a point that will be the center of the topmost ball of foliage.

The spectral quality of these tiered yew standards, poised as though about to drift off, owes much to the subdued wintry light. Another reason for their curious weightlessness is the absence of a bottom tier to ground level. In this garden it may be that setting these tiers against an open landscape is more important than closing in the view with solid shapes anchored to the ground. The area kept clear at the base of each trunk simplifies mowing and reduces the competition from grass for nutrients and water.

TRAINING A BOXWOOD SPIRAL

MATERIALS REQUIRED

A vigorous, small-leaved boxwood (*Buxus sempervirens*) with a straight and vertical leader, trimmed as a cone to a height of approximately 4ft (1.2m)—whether container-grown or planted in the open garden, the specimen should have been established for about a year before being shaped as a spiral

Tape

Shears; hand pruners

1 In early summer, before shaping, wind broad tape around the specimen to mark out the upper edge of four turns of a well- and regularly spaced spiral.

2 Using hand pruners, make small cuts into the cone to serve as guide marks along the upper edge of the line of the tape. (A)

3 Remove the tape and, using hand pruners, cut the leader (if this has not already been done when it was trimmed to a cone) and then cut growths back to the main stem along the guide-mark line.

A   B   C

4 Wind tape around the specimen again, this time using it to indicate the lower edge of the turns, and then cut guide marks.

5 Remove the tape and, following the guide marks, cut growths back to the main stem. (B)

6 Using shears, trim the upper and lower surfaces of the turns of the spiral, giving them rounded, not sharp, edges. (C)

7 In the following and subsequent years, trim in early and late summer with shears.

It is clear from old gardening manuals that many more complex tiered arrangements were once popular, a single specimen sometimes consisting of several different shapes stacked one above the other. It is not easy to place this extravagant kind of geometry in the garden, and although the method to follow in carving out the tiers is the same as that used for creating a succession of disks or balls, maintaining a range of neat and well-balanced shapes on a single stem is a great test of the gardener's eye and hand.

Spirals

The spiral is a most attractive geometric topiary shape which, with its tapering and gently swirling turns, conveys a sense of languorous movement. It is sometimes suggested that a spiral should be formed by training the pliable stem of a young yew or boxwood around a stout stake; but a less problematic method, and the one usually practiced, is to train the main stem of a plant vertically and to carve the turns of the spiral out of growth that

has been clipped to form a cone. The plant to be shaped must have a sturdy and vertical main stem and should be well developed. The turns of the spiral should not be too close; otherwise shading will result in thin growth. When the spiral is first shaped there will almost certainly be gaps in the most recent growth, so that the turns do not seem completely regular. New shoots and foliage will fill out these gaps and regular trimming will encourage dense growth, although as a result of shading the underside of the turns may often be less leafy than the upper surface. You can begin to train a young plant that has not yet reached the desired height but in this case you should leave the leader to keep growing. The spiral is a shape that warrants being kept neat and well defined. Once the plant has reached the desired height, it is worth trimming it twice in the growing season, at least in the first two years.

OPPOSITE Small-leaved ivies trained on wire frames and boxwood spirals, balls and cones lined up on each side of a path mark a point of transition.

Animal shapes in topiary

ABOVE The animation of a hungry snail in boxwood is suggested by the offset curve of the neck and head.

OPPOSITE Harvey S. Ladew developed the Ladew Topiary Gardens at Monkton, Maryland, between 1929 and 1976, and was inspired to create this hunting scene after seeing hedge-top topiary of a foxhunt in England.

Some connoisseurs of topiary are disparaging about the representation of living shapes in clipped greenery, but this aspect of the craft, recorded right back in the first accounts of topiary, has been a source of innocent pleasure to countless topiarists and the vast numbers of their—sometimes slightly puzzled—admirers. Nevertheless it is as well for the novice to understand at the outset that representation in topiary has severe limitations. Clipped greenery, even with plants such as boxwood and yew that produce a dense surface of small leaves, is not a medium that readily conveys animated figures, detailed finish or subtle modeling. It comes into its own when shapes can be reduced to broad simple forms while still conveying a strong generalized impression or a caricature-like exaggeration. It is not surprising, therefore, that much representational topiary is either a looming presence in the garden or light-heartedly comic.

The growth pattern of plants is such that, unless more than one plant is used to make a shape, it is difficult to divide the base into two or more legs. It is, of course, possible to use stems of a plant as a kind of armature for the topiary, as has been done in the well-known hunting scene at the Ladew Topiary Gardens, Maryland, in which a pack of hounds race across the lawn followed by a mounted huntsman who is about to take a fence. As a general rule, however, it is best to create a shape with a broad base or else one that is logically supported by a single stem.

Furthermore, since the strong natural tendency of plants is to grow upward, extensions growing in a different direction need to be coaxed. This is not so difficult if it is simply a matter of encouraging a short length of growth to extend beyond a compact body at an angle somewhere between the horizontal and the vertical. Light canes can be used to do this, as is recommended to form the beak and tail of a nesting bird (see page 54). It is even possible to encourage a slender growth to extend further in a more or less horizontal position by tying it to a cane or by suspending a weight from it on a string, as is sometimes done when training an extension such as the elegant slender tail of a topiary pheasant. However, forcing a large section of a plant to grow down, as would be necessary to form the hanging head of an animal, fights against the plant's natural tendency. You can achieve the best results by

A TOPIARY NESTING BIRD SHAPED IN BOXWOOD

A

B

C

D

These instructions are for shaping a bird on a nest-like pedestal with a total height of about 20in (50cm). It is intended for planting in the open garden, but you could complete the early stages of training while the plant is growing in a container. If the shape is to be grown permanently in a container, it would look better-proportioned with the pedestal reduced to a rim about 4in (10cm) high. A pleasing contrast of textures may be achieved by trimming the bird twice annually, in early and late summer, but the pedestal only in late summer.

MATERIALS REQUIRED

A bushy, small-leaved boxwood (*Buxus sempervirens*) about 18in (45cm) high, preferably without a strong central leader but with stems that can be trained to left and right

Light canes about 30in (75cm) long; tarred string

Shears; hand pruners

1 In early summer, begin shaping by trimming the pedestal, aiming to form a cylinder 8in (20cm) high and 12in (30cm) in diameter. (A)
2 At the same time, begin to shape the bird: first decide which stems will be used to form the head and tail and then cut away excess growth. To hold the selected stems at the required angle, insert two canes and tie the appropriate stem to each with tarred string. (B)
3 In late summer of the same year, trim the bird and pedestal again,

shaping the head roughly into a dome with some strands protruding for the beak, and the tail into an elongated cone. Check the ties, loosening them if they are constricting the stems. (C)
4 In the following and subsequent summers, continue trimming and check the ties regularly. Once the stems have set in position and the beak and tail are nearly formed, the canes, if possible, should be removed. (D)

---

taking account of the way plants grow and training compact, usually broad-based shapes with a minimum of short extensions, which should be either horizontal or tilted upward.

To the keen topiarist these considerations are not limitations but a challenge, to be met by designing a suitable animal form and then shaping it from a living plant or plants. Help in the design often comes from plants themselves, with quirks of shape and growth suggesting a form that is struggling to get out. The alternative is to place heavy reliance on frames, generally of metal, using a small-leaved malleable plant such as *Ligustrum delavayanum* to complete the shape in green.

Bird, human and animal shapes
Birds are probably the most widely represented natural forms in topiary. This is partly because a generalized idea of a bird with its legs tucked under it can be reduced to a simple combination of two spherical shapes, one large for the body, the other small for the head, with a short extension for a beak and a longer extension for the tail. However, the generalized bird is less familiar in topiary than several distinctive and familiar types of birds. The peacock, fanning its tail with hyperbolic vanity, is one of the most popular of all the complex topiary shapes. With this bird, as with all representational topiary, anatomical accuracy is not what counts.

Only the most literal-minded will quibble if a peacock may barely be distinguished from a male turkey. A mature specimen does not need supports but, while you are developing the shape of the tail as a regular fan, you need to tie growths to supports set at the appropriate angle. Check all ties carefully from time to time and loosen them if they have become too tight.

Ducks and hens are other familiar bird shapes that lend themselves to topiary of modest size. A rooster offers the potential for a more ambitious shape (as in the garden illustrated on page 59). It is tempting to make something of the distinctive comb and wattle, but the general rule applies: rather than focus on detail, it is better to make a broad effect that is easy to maintain.

Birds of prey are also highly distinctive in outline and their heraldic associations make them appropriate subjects for the grand garden. Your model should be highly stylized: one of the many depictions of the Horus falcon of Ancient Egypt, for instance, including sculptural versions in which the legs and tail form a unified mass. The shape can be trimmed from a modified column, as can a delightfully inappropriate garden resident, the penguin, permanently alert with its beak tilted upward.

The problem with all animal topiary is subordinating anatomical accuracy to the creation of simple shapes that are easily grasped visually. It is not surprising, therefore, that one of the most popular topiary shapes is that of the teddy bear, for which the model is already stylized. The standard topiary teddy bear has short legs extending horizontally, which gets over the problem presented by the legs of most quadrupeds, except low-slung ones, such as mice or rabbits. Such compact shapes make delightful topiary for containers. For large stylized animals a position at rest, with the legs tucked under, provides a suitably broad-based shape. You could form a splendid lion about 6½ft (2m) high and 8–10ft (2.5–3m) long from two yew trees planted along its length. Provided they are of the same clone, the yews will merge so that they may soon be treated as a single plant consistent in color and texture. Another solution is a stylized version of an animal sitting on its hind legs with the topiary shape absorbing the forelegs. Sleek cats as portrayed in Ancient Egyptian art provide superb models for the feline quartet in the garden illustrated on page 109.

The leader of a boxwood bush has been trained up through a first tier, forming a nest-like shape, and cut back to encourage dense growth, shaped as a barrel-chested rooster. The comb and tail cannot be left untrimmed indefinitely but they add a life-like touch.

There is scope for experimentation in the clipping of columns topped by animal heads, an adaptation of decorative finials in architecture and furniture. Again, the key to success lies in reducing the anatomy of animals and birds such as lions, rams, Minoan bulls, eagles or even unicorns to very simple forms. There are plenty of examples from the sculpture of many periods and cultures to provide guides. From vigorous yew columns clipped to shape you could create a magnificent avenue of heraldic beasts.

A two-phase clipping regime ensures that this lion in golden yew can show off his mane throughout most of the summer. All but the mane can be trimmed in early summer and the whole lion in late summer.

Unlike animal shapes, the human figure has been rather neglected as a subject for topiary, the urge to portray it as fully animated or with complex modeling perhaps being defeated by the medium. Limbs inevitably pose a problem. It is difficult to think of a topiary human figure in which the feet are not together and the arms held in to the sides. However, there is more scope for experimentation than is generally attempted, and an ambitious gardener might like to try some of the ideas suggested here.

Distinctive dress might provide a suitably bold shape for a standing figure. The crinoline is ideal for this purpose and it could be strikingly topped by a spherical head with a tilted hat. You could create the slightly sinister impression of a figure in a floor-length cape by cutting a wedge out of a cone as the opening of the cape, revealing the figure as another cone inside. A bulbous off-center hat might confirm that this was a knight companion of the Garter. A triumphant ballet dancer about to take her bow is a subject with

more éclat. The figure on points could rise as a bare stem to a conical tutu, and above it a neat cylindrical body topped by a small rounded head with arms raised from the body. You would need to support the arms with canes to train them. Seated and stooping figures have the advantage of being broad-based. The quiet murmur of a timeless conversation might be suggested by a pair of seated figures simply modeled and leaning toward one another. A broad-based rounded shape as the body with a small sphere as the head and an upward-reaching arm could be the ideal gardening companion, weatherbeaten but reliable in all weathers.

The bust—the head and shoulders set on a living pedestal—is an alternative to the full figure, but without an exaggerated feature, such as Cyrano de Bergerac's nose or some highly distinctive headgear, there is the risk of the portrait being blankly anonymous. The crown and elegantly elongated neck of Nefertiti, Queen of Ancient Egypt, provides just the kind of recognizable shape that

A FABULOUS BEAST IN YEW

A

B

C

D

The extensions of limb and tail and the reversed head make the support of canes necessary during the formative pruning of this heraldic beast. These instructions are for a specimen with a total height of 5ft (1.5m), and a somewhat low pedestal, which may be reasonably finished in five to eight years. A pedestal 40in (1m) high, broader at the base than at the top, would make an even more impressive finished effect and would not take much longer to shape if the yew were slightly larger at the initial stage. Some modeling is necessary to give the beast character. The forelegs, held together, head and tail all need to be narrower than the body.

MATERIALS REQUIRED

A bushy yew (*Taxus baccata*) 30–40in (75–100cm) in height, which has been initially trained and lightly shaped to square the base, and has had the leader removed

2 canes about 10ft (3m) long and another about 5ft (1.5m) long; tarred string

Shears; hand pruners

1 In early summer, shape the pedestal to form the beginning of a rectangular block approximately 20in (50cm) high and about 40in (1m) deep and wide, but at this stage do not trim the top growth. Insert into the pedestal two long canes angled for training the legs and body of the beast so that they converge at a height of about 40in (1m). Tie them together with a third shorter cane as a crosspiece to give strength and to provide support for growths that will be

trained to make the tail. Working toward the shape of the beast, tie stems into the canes and trim away unwanted growth. (A)

2 In late fall of the same year, trim again. (B)

3 In summer of the following and subsequent years, trim twice, tying in growth as required and checking established ties, loosening them if they are too tight. (C)

4 Remove the canes when the shape is well established, with the tail and head wholly or partly formed. (D)

---

lends itself to topiary; a stylized version of the head and shoulders supported on a pedestal clipped from the same plant would make a solemnly arresting feature in a garden. Another candidate for this kind of treatment is Napoleon in his two-cornered hat. A sultan, head wrapped in a turban, and a doge, wearing *il corno*, the cap of office, would make a less personalized but intriguing pair.

The telamon and caryatid, stone columns in the form of male and female figures, are classical architectural features that have been much used as sculptural components in gardens since the

Renaissance. They might be recreated as topiary, their effect being achieved more by the rhythmic repetition of the simple shapes than by the detail. For a really ambitious scheme you could take inspiration from the gardens of the Palazzo Farnese at Caprarola in Italy. There a late-16th-century parterre is haunted by the urn-bearing telemons and caryatids that surround it and fix their unblinking gaze over its boxwood compartments. The mysterious serenity of this garden might well survive in a scaled-down adaptation with figures in topiary.

Rooster topiary in a small garden

A rooster in yew provides the focal point for the small walled garden opposite, only 20ft (6m) by 16ft (5m) in extent. The rooster is centered on the point of entry into the garden but cannot be approached directly. The pleasure of discovering that he is a family man with two wives and several offspring (all shaped in boxwood) is reserved for those who make their way to an area of decking. Partly shaded by an arbor and its trained grapevine, the decking is slightly elevated, 6–8in (15–20cm) above the gravel mulch through which the yew and boxwood topiary grows. From here the impression is that behind a bed planted with two dome-shaped bay laurels and aromatic herbs sprinkled with bright poppies is a sunny little yard in which poultry busily scratch about for food.

A more conventional use of topiary in this garden is the row of five boxwood blocks, the tops shaped as pyramids; it is planted in gravel between the house and a narrow pool, edged with granite paving blocks, that extends the full width of the garden. A decking bridge spans the water, beside which is a bed filled with moisture-loving perennials. The paved path that runs across the garden has at one end a round-topped slab of yew crowned with a bird and at the other a wooden tub filled with long-flowering plants. The garden is finished with trellis panels, set out slightly from the walls and supporting a mixture of climbers, including clematis and roses, that provide flowers thoughout the summer. The area directly behind the rooster has been left clear so that nothing takes away from the bold shape of the lordly bird. The small, curiously propeller-like, white flowers of *Trachelospermum jasminoides* fill the garden with a heavenly scent for many weeks in summer.

With relatively small changes, this garden could be adapted to form a compartment within a larger scheme. For example, the walls could be replaced by trellis and the paved path extended through openings in one or both directions. Even in a very different garden the easily recognized shapes of roosters, hens and chickens make appealing subjects to shape in yew and boxwood.

LEFT A rooster and his small flock of hens and chickens, some no more than blobs, stray onto a lawn. Much of the effect is achieved by the highly naturalistic grouping of these very simple shapes in boxwood.

N

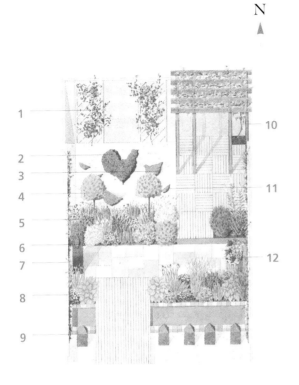

1 1 of 2 wall-trained climbing roses
2 Topiary rooster in yew
3 1 of 2 topiary hens in boxwood
4 1 of 2 standard bay laurels
5 Bed of annual and perennial herbs
  and flowering annuals
6 Topiary yew slab with bird finial
7 1 of 2 lengths of trellis planted with
  a mixture of climbers, including
  Trachelospermum jasminoides and
  various clematis
8 Bed of moisture-loving perennials
9 1 of 5 topiary blocks with pyramid
  tops trimmed from boxwood
10 Grapevine trained on arbor
11 1 of 3 topiary chickens in boxwood
12 Wooden tub with seasonal planting
   including heliotrope (*Heliotropium*
   'Marine')

Approximately 20ft (6m) by 16ft (5m)

ABOVE LEFT This mysterious female figure in yew suggests a garden haunted by beings magically immobilized as topiary who wait for something more than a regular trim to be revitalized as flesh and blood.

ABOVE RIGHT Toy-like figures rising above an interesting grouping of dome-like topiary shapes are reminiscent of the Walt Disney characters portrayed in living plants at Disneyland in California.

LEFT A privet stag is permanently arrested in its flight through the garden.

ABOVE Their growth is patchy and they need a trim, but these long-stemmed birds shaped in *Ligustrum delavayanum* have a liveliness often lacking in more studied and scrupulously maintained topiary.

RIGHT The extravagant tail of the peacock, a bird introduced to Europe long ago but unmistakably exotic, has made it a favorite subject for topiary. This bird is shaped in yew, with its tail gracefully lowered rather than, as is more common, stiffly fanned.

Fantasy topiary

Beyond the familiar vocabulary of geometric shapes and a bestiary of more or less recognizable creatures, topiary takes two quite different directions. In one it light-heartedly extends its representational role to include an astonishing range of inanimate objects. In the other, it follows a course into less well-charted waters, finding shapes that have their own intrinsic interest or beauty, and new ways to place these in contexts more varied than the rectilinear layouts associated with conventional topiary.

Whimsical topiary

We know from the Roman writer Pliny the Elder that as early as the 1st century A.D. plants were ingeniously shaped to represent inanimate as well as living things. The Romans, one suspects, took a rather earnest view of this kind of topiary, as have some more recent gardeners sometimes, too. But classical porticoes and rustic cabins, sailing ships and gondolas, automobiles and locomotives, teapots and coffee jugs—a few of the many topiary subjects attempted— are undeniably most endearing when they come across as expressions of playful *joie de vivre*. Their geniality, the originality of their invention and the commitment to their development over years make it easy to view them with aesthetic judgment suspended.

The whimsical shapes that are most easily assimilated in the garden are compact and regular in outline, often little more than slight elaborations of simple geometric shapes. However, to make a sensation, nothing short of an improbable achievement of verisimilitude will do: the strings of a harp, for instance, or the sails of a ship.

In Renaissance gardens the most ambitious shapes were made by training all manner of plants over frameworks of withies (willow

LEFT A large-scale leafy steam engine is in itself a surprising discovery in a garden; the confrontation of engine and manned gondola is surreal. As privet is fast-growing, these shapes could be developed relatively quickly from numerous bushes planted close together.

OPPOSITE The common yew is an exceptionally versatile evergreen for large-scale topiary and it will hold its shape well with one trim annually. The techniques for training geometric, representational and freeform shapes are essentially the same.

LEFT Here the topiarist, while trimming a squat and obese boxwood bush, seems to have discovered complex natural folding in the raw material.

OPPOSITE When viewed individually most of the ornamented domes making up this magnificent avenue of trimmed yew seem to be drawn from a repertoire of familiar topiary shapes. The fantasy is in the scale of the undertaking and the highly original character that each specimen has acquired.

lashing). It seems likely that some of these creations did not last long; not only would the willow supports have needed replacing after a few seasons, but many of the plants used would now be thought quite unsuitable. Modern frames are made sometimes of wood but more usually of metal. Several plants can be used to make large pieces of topiary, and to complete a piece quickly the fast-growing privet is often preferred to the relatively slow-growing yew and boxwood. Inevitably, shapes in privet need frequent trimming if they are to be kept neat.

Before embarking on a large-scale but light-hearted piece, it is worth considering how far you want the jaunty tone to extend in your garden. Compartmentalizing the whimsy may make it possible to create a garden that reflects more than one mood.

Freeform topiary
An indication of the versatility and longevity of the craft of topiary, which has been practiced for centuries with a relatively limited range of shapes, is that it can still be applied today, using more imaginative shapes. Some of the shapes might be freshly minted; others could be inspired by natural forms, products of technology, traditional and modern crafts or the output of countless artists.

The sampler and its commentary on page 67 give some indication of the variety of forms that might be attempted. All lend themselves to being clipped out of classic topiary plants such as boxwood and yew, and present no more difficulties than simple geometric shapes. Although not familiar as topiary, the shapes are easy to read and straightforward to maintain. Their simplicity is to some extent deceptive, for in almost every case the shape creates an interesting, sometimes dramatic, play of light and shade. In creating new forms in topiary, devising easily maintained shapes that exploit the play of light is a profitable line to pursue.

Most of the shapes could fit quite happily in gardens with formal layouts but could stand just as comfortably in less rigorously ordered settings. Freeing topiary from conventional geometric patterns is one way of allowing us to see interesting shapes with a fresh look. Well-considered juxtapositions can enhance the value of simple shapes, and there are infinite possibilities for varied and pleasing groupings that suggest organic connections more subtle than those of tyrannical symmetry.

The technique of cloud pruning is more commonly practiced in parts of Asia, where it originated, and in the United States than in Europe. Pruning and trimming result in an exposed and simplified structure of branches terminating in tight leafy masses. Symmetry is inappropriate but, as with this juniper, the shape must have a natural equilibrium.

Cloud pruning

The traditional Asian technique of cloud pruning, which is increasingly popular in Western gardens, is another departure from conventional topiary. The aim is to reveal the underlying structure of the plant, unwanted growth being cut away to show the trunk and branches, which support cloud-like puffs of clipped foliage. The choice of plant is important: the woody framework must be characterful and the plant must also tolerate regular clipping. A favorite for the purpose is the Chinese juniper (*Juniperus chinensis*); other junipers and various mainly coniferous trees and shrubs can also be used. Although cloud pruning is a much less severe technique than bonsai, in which pruning maintains an apparently natural but miniaturized shape, there are similarities, particularly in the artfulness that is sometimes needed to eliminate branches and stems to create an idealized framework. The non-geometric shape that is the result makes it suitable for informal gardens.

ABSTRACT AND FREEFORM SAMPLER

A suitable plant and workable dimensions are proposed for each shape illustrated, but even in these examples there is considerable scope for interesting variations of scale and modifications to dimensions. You can use taut lines or formers as guides to creating and maintaining the shapes; the quantity and spacing of plants will depend on the scale required.

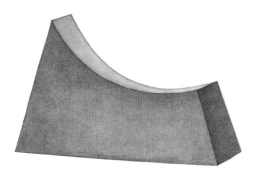

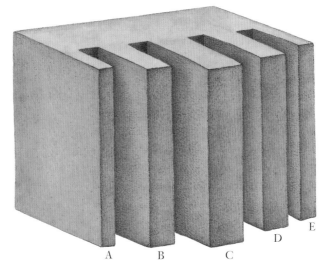

4 Among the simplest of interlocking shapes are those formed by hedge-like lengths of clipped green intersecting at right angles. The semicircular cuts at the center of this example would show to best effect if the shape were seen from above. Boxwood (*Buxus sempervirens* 'Handsworthiensis'), h. 40in (1m), w. of each plane 5ft (1.5m), d. 12in (30cm), dia. of semicircular cut-out 20in (50cm).

1 A circular bite taken from a wedge makes the incomplete shape more interesting than the full slice. A pair in this shape running parallel or in line, the taller ends closest to each other, would have the force of greatly simplified heraldic beasts. Yew (*Taxus baccata*), h. 5ft (1.5m), w. 6½ft (2m), d. 40in (1m) at base, 24in (60cm) at apex.

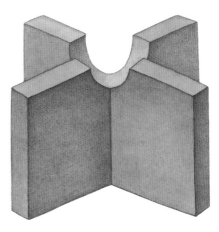

2 Projections of different width and depth extend from a simple hedge-like cube to form a symmetrical facade on which there is a dramatic play of light and shade. Yew (*Taxus baccata*), main shape: h. 5ft (1.5m), w. 6ft (1.8m), d. 24in (60cm); projections: (A and E) w. 6in (15cm), d. 12in (30cm), (B and D) w. 8in (20cm), d. 18in (45cm), (C) w. 12in (30cm), d. 24in (60cm); distance between projections 8in (20cm).

5 The superimposition of two reduced versions of the outline shape create a shell-like form, which is marked by strong shadows when lit from the side. Boxwood (*Buxus sempervirens* 'Handsworthiensis'), h. 30in (75cm), w. 4ft (1.2m), max. d. at base 12in (30cm), each superimposed shape 2in (5cm) deep.

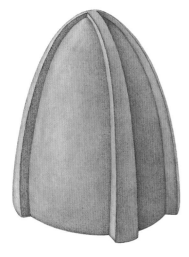

3 An egg shape, cut across at the base, seems to be held down by straps or flanges. You could plant one on the scale suggested here in a plain pot slightly raised to make a powerful focal point in a bed or garden compartment. The use of variegated boxwood would give a light touch. Boxwood (*Buxus sempervirens* 'Elegantissima'), h. 30in (75cm), dia. of the egg shape 16in (40cm), dia. including flanges 18in (45cm).

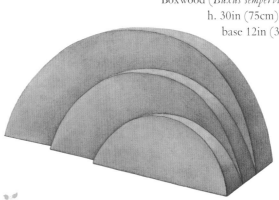

Changing moods of topiary

The contrasts between the topiary in the two compartments of this small garden help to keep interest alive through all the seasons.

A hedge of beech (*Fagus sylvatica*) forms the far boundary—the garden is approximately 37ft (11.5m) by 20ft (6m)—while panels of trellis painted pale gray extend the side walls to a height of 8ft (2.5m) and partly screen two compartments from each other. The smaller compartment, nearest the house, is paved with blue-tinted brick, while the compartment behind has a gravel floor with carpet-like areas of brick paving.

The first compartment, which is approached from the house by a side door or through French windows, has an informal air. There are no flower beds except for narrow strips at the base of the trellis, planted with a scarlet-flowering Japanese quince (*Chaenomeles* x *superba* 'Rowallane'). But the area lends itself to container gardening, an interesting medley including potted topiary and distinctive shrubs such as skimmia and seasonal combinations of bulbs, annuals and perennials. In summer the containers can be moved to the periphery of the area, leaving space for furnishing with table and chairs for relaxed living outdoors, and frequent traffic through the garden. Using several examples of paired topiary, such as the domes of Portugal laurel and boxwood spirals, a lightly formal touch can be combined with looser arrangements, easily reorganized as plants come into their prime or fade. In winter the furniture is removed and the containers regrouped so that they show to handsome effect when seen from inside. In very late winter, even when the earliest flowers are beginning to show, topiary forms the main display.

Through the trellis a narrow gap between a pair of arc-like segments in yew provides a glimpse of the mysteriously calm second compartment. These clipped yews and another pair, shape reversed, create a mazy approach to the ramp, which leads to a throne- or altar-like shape in yew. This shape stands on a low platform below the arched beech hedge, which is coppery in winter, mid-green in summer. Red winter-flowering pansies could be replaced in summer by annual impatiens, either white or of a single intense color.

LEFT Hoarfrost glistening in the sunshine adds winter glamor to the twiggy heads of the early Dutch honeysuckle (*Lonicera periclymenum* 'Belgica'). The formal shapes of these standards are in marked contrast to the unruly growth of the plant as a climber.

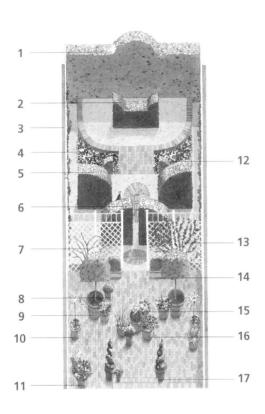

N

1   Beech hedge
2   Topiary shape in yew
3   1 of 2 lengths of trellis
     supporting ivies
4   1 of 2 beds seasonally planted
     with winter-flowering pansies
5   1 of 2 topiary shapes in yew
6   1 of 2 topiary shapes in yew,
     the same as 5 but reversed
7   Climbing rose
8   1 of 2 pot-grown topiary
     balls in boxwood
9   1 of 2 pot-grown standards
     of Portugal laurel
10 1 of 2 pot-grown standards
     of *Cotoneaster salicifolius*
     'Pendulus'

11 Pot planted with *Skimmia
     japonica* 'Rubella' and
     S. j. subsp. *reevesiana*
12 1 of 2 topiary shapes in
     boxwood
13 Fan-trained Japanese quince
     (*Chaenomeles × superba*
     'Rowallane')
14 1 of 2 container-grown
     topiary shapes in boxwood
15 Pot-grown topiary dome in
     boxwood
16 1 of 7 pots with plants of
     interest for foliage or flowers
     in late winter or early spring
17 1 of 2 pot-grown topiary
     spirals in boxwood

Approximately 37ft (11.5m) by 20ft (6m)

Plant sculpture with ivy

The versatility of several mainly climbing plants makes it possible to create attractive and amusing shapes by training them on frames set in containers. A small-leaved plant closely enveloping a shape creates an impression similar to that achieved with conventional topiary but the finished state is reached more quickly. Common or English ivy (*Hedera helix*), which is evergreen and remarkably hardy, is the outstanding plant for this purpose, and also for training on walls and the ground. It is best known as an ornamental in its juvenile stage, when the stems normally cling to surfaces by means of aerial roots. In the adult stage, when flowers and fruit are produced, the stems at the top of the plant do not have aerial roots and the leaves growing from them do not have lobes. Common ivy has numerous cultivars, which show considerable variations in vigor as well as leaf size, shape and color. A selection of ivies for training as shapes is given in the Directory (Plants for Special Purposes, page 154). Where the climate is warm enough, the creeping fig (*Ficus pumila*) is another good plant for training because of its close-hugging growth.

Wall and ground-level designs in ivy

Ivy is such a tough and versatile plant that it can often be used decoratively even in the shade where few other plants would thrive. As a self-clinging climber it can be guided and trimmed to form two-dimensional designs on walls. In a paved garden it needs only small gaps at the base of walls for planting. One option in a walled garden is green *trompe-l'oeil*, trimming ivy to create simple architectural shapes such as columns and obelisks. Grid and diaper (diamond-repeating) patterns are best outlined on wires attached to vine eyes; the ivy is trained up, tied in position and then trimmed as it grows and clings to the wall. A chalked outline is a useful guide for fanciful shapes, most effective when they are simple, bold silhouettes.

You can also use trained ivy to define architectural shapes, making, for instance, a green screen of sturdy grid-patterned trellis. You can go even further, with simple structures in wood or trellis providing the base for a green architecture of pavilions and arbors. Ivy is particularly well suited to training as swags, perhaps

LEFT Although appearing to hang in heavy festoons, these ivies are trained up from ground level between the trunks of pleached trees—perhaps like the ivy hanging in swags between the plane trees surrounding the hippodrome in the garden of his Tuscan villa that Pliny the Younger described in the 1st century A.D.

OPPOSITE A severe grid of ivy trained on a metal frame backs a stone bench, from which there is a view of a parterre with dwarf boxwood hedges. Eventually the ivy will make a shading canopy.

TWO BALLS OF IVY ON A METAL FRAME

The following instructions are for planting ivy on a commercially produced frame consisting of two wire spheres, one above the other. Ivy can be planted at almost any time of the year but the advantage of planting in early spring is the long growing season that follows, in which case, with regular watering and feeding, the ivy will have covered part if not all of the second ball within eighteen months.

MATERIALS REQUIRED

A terra-cotta or other heavy pot about 16in (40cm) across and high, and with a broad base

A soil-based compost

A galvanized wire frame consisting of two balls, one above the other, the lower one about 16in (40cm) in diameter and the upper one about 12in (30cm), and a pronged base

2–3 young plants of a small-leaved cultivar of the common ivy (*Hedera helix*)

Soft string

Hand pruners or scissors

A

B

C

1 In late winter, fill the container with compost to within about ¾in (2cm) of the rim and then set the frame temporarily in position, marking planting positions for two or three ivy plants.
2 Remove the frame, plant the ivies and then set the frame back in position. (If the lower ball of the frame stands well above the compost, planting can be done with the frame in position.) (A)
3 Tie short growths of the ivies to the frame, spreading them evenly around the base. Shorten any long stems that are sparsely furnished with leaves, cutting them back to compact growth.
4 As the shoots of the ivy extend, tie them into the frame so that the lower ball is evenly covered.
5 When the plants are big enough, train three or four stems up the support of the second ball, cutting others back, and tie in growths evenly. (B)
6 As the plants grow during subsequent months, maintain the shape by trimming away excessive growth and removing dead leaves. (C)

as part of a grander architectural scheme, or more simply trained up posts and then along linking chains.

The dense evergreen foliage of ivies that makes them such a versatile ground cover can be put to good use in creating patterns and designs to floor a garden. Prime sites for this kind of treatment are sunken shady areas or ground under formally planted trees. You can create the pattern with narrow beds in paving, preferably slightly raised, and plant them up with ivy. Or you can lay out a design, either geometric or fanciful, in a bed and elaborate it by contrasting ivies of different leaf color. You could base the design on knots and conventional motifs such as the *fleur de lis*, but there is nothing like an original stencil design or geometric pattern to give a garden a distinctive character. Ivies need regular trimming if the outlines of a design are to remain sharp.

Ivy on frames

Commercially produced galvanized wire frames fall into two broad categories. Some are two-dimensional shapes, at their simplest just a hoop but often jokey silhouettes to be filled in by the trained plant. Three-dimensional shapes, ranging from geometric balls and

In an ambitious set piece, ivy ponies trot tirelessly around a boxwood-edged ring. Although the metal frames outline simple, bold shapes, they have been created with a real sense of the movement of the animals. On this scale it has been possible to use a vigorous and large-leaved cultivar of the common ivy (*Hedera helix*) as the green cladding.

cones to stylized representations of birds and animals, are much more useful. A frame must include a pronged or U-shaped base, covered with compost when the shape is in position. A shortcoming of some frames is that the bases are too insubstantial to give the planted shape stability. Pushing the prongs into crosspieces of styrofoam cut to fit into the base of a container will help make the planted shape secure. The container must have the right proportions for its frame and be deep enough to accommodate the part of the frame covered by compost. Drainage holes are essential and weight is important so that the finished shape is not top-heavy. Broad-based terra-cotta pots are well suited to this.

Even self-clinging plants such as ivy are unable to attach themselves to wire supports, so plants have to be trained by

Even small-leaved ivies trained closely cannot convey detail—a point to bear in mind if you are making your own frames out of chicken wire for training ivy. Simple bird shapes, such as these, are among the easiest for the amateur to make.

twining, weaving and tying. Twining and weaving are satisfactory techniques to use on plants with reasonably long stems and particularly good for hoops or hearts of flowering climbers such as the half-hardy jasmine *Jasminum polyanthum*. With ivy, on a fairly open frame, such as most of those that are produced commercially, twining and weaving alone are unlikely to produce a really closely covered shape, and usually have to be combined with a certain amount of tying. Ties, made with soft string or raffia, should be loose enough to allow stems to expand; if they cause constriction, they should be cut and retied. With ivy it is tempting to use well-established plants with long stems in order to get the shape well covered at the outset; however, you can achieve a denser effect by using young plants and keeping the growth short-jointed. Cutting back any long stems that are thinly furnished with leaves will

encourage the development of new shoots which can be tied in to create an even outline.

For the imaginative gardener, the pure kitsch or predictable good taste of commercially made shapes cannot compete with original designs. What you can make yourself depends on your practical skills. You can cut No. 10 or even heavier-gauge galvanized wire to size and bend it using wire-cutters and pliers, but any joins will need to be twist-tied or soldered. Even without soldering it is possible to make a useful and pleasing shape with a chicken-wire skin molded around a wire skeleton. Chicken wire is a surprisingly versatile material that can be worked into a wide range of shapes. The closeness of the mesh makes it easy to combine weaving of short-jointed shoots and tying so that the foliage cover eventually hugs the carcass loosely. Clear lines and broad forms

TWO IVY RABBITS ON CHICKEN-WIRE FRAMES

These instructions are for planting ivy on frames consisting of wire framework supporting a chicken-wire skin. Each rabbit outline (heights given below) consists of two spherical shapes: one larger one attached to a smaller one as the head, with extensions for ears and a tail.

MATERIALS REQUIRED

A terra-cotta or other heavy and broad-based pot about 16in (40cm) across and 12in (30cm) high

A soil-based compost

Two frames made of chicken wire on a galvanized wire armature, one about 16in (40cm) high, the other about 12in (30cm) high, excluding the extensions that allow the frames to stand firm in the pot

5–6 young plants of a small-leaved cultivar of the common ivy (*Hedera helix*)

Soft string

Hand pruners or scissors

1 In late winter, fill the container with compost to within about ¾in (2cm) of the rim and then set the frames in position, anchoring them securely in the soil.
2 Plant the ivies, one on each side of the small rabbit, three around the large rabbit. (A)

3 Cut back long shoots with few leaves to a joint near the base.
4 Tie short growths of the ivies to the frame with the string, spreading them evenly around the base, and work longer growths in and out of the holes in the chicken wire.
5 As the shoots of the ivy plants

extend, tie them in or work them in and out of the chicken wire, keeping the two shapes distinct. (B)
6 When the rabbits are completely covered with foliage, maintain the shape by regularly trimming away excessive growth and removing dead leaves. (C)

make the most satisfactory topiary shapes but these can be composed of several components joined together, such as sphere on sphere to create a body on a head.

Stuffed frames

Stuffed frames are increasingly popular for decorations in the home or conservatory and some public gardens have impressive indoor and outdoor displays. Plants are trained up from below or inserted directly into a moisture-retaining material enclosed by a wire or chicken-wire frame. The plants root and spread their foliage over the shape and as they develop they are trained: growths are pinned into place if necessary (hairpins are useful for this) and trimmed.

The material generally recommended for the stuffing is sphagnum moss, used like a wrapping around a soilless compost.

Sphagnum moss is easy to handle, takes up water freely and holds it well. There is, however, concern about the environmental damage resulting from its collection. Most of the fibrous liners used for hanging baskets can be used in its place but they need more regular watering or dampening than sphagnum moss to maintain satisfactory moisture levels. The extensive range of plants that can be grown indoors includes climbers and trailers such as ivies, creeping plants such as baby's tears (*Soleirolia soleirolia*), numerous succulents, and shaggy and spiky plants such as the spider plant (*Chlorophytum comosum*). When the technique is used outdoors, the main problem is that it requires the most devoted watering by hand when there is no irrigation and dampening system. Ivies are among the best plants to use on account of their toughness and hardiness.

Long-lived topiary

Surviving topiary in old well-documented gardens is proof that specimens shaped out of plants such as boxwood, Italian cypress and yew can be very long-lived. Pests and diseases are facts of life and take their toll (see plant entries in the Directory, page 148), but it is shifts of fashion and neglect that account for major losses.

Common problems

Some problems are short-lived. Superficial frost or wind damage will grow out, and you can remove the scorched growths when clipping. Gaps can be expected on young plants and will generally fill quite naturally as the plants mature. Branches that have been pushed out of place can be tied back with tarred string. Holes in established specimens are slow to fill but it is often possible to train in replacement shoots; it is best to leave these untrimmed for a season to gain length and then tie them into position before shortening them to encourage dense growth. However, in the case of a dead branch, removal may be so devastating to a shape that dramatic remodeling is the best solution.

You can often rectify loss of shape even after a break of several years in the clipping regime, although you may have to approach the specimen in the same way as a previously untrimmed plant that has within it a form waiting to be discovered. The quirkish shapes and wavy patterns of growth that old topiary specimens sometimes acquire can be endearing but also make trimming back into a more regular shape more difficult. It is often better to live with a deformed peacock or the like than attempt reshaping. On variegated plants, growths sometimes revert to green and develop at the expense of the variegated cultivar, creating a distorted shape. The ideal solution is to cut out the part that has reverted but it may be more practical to abandon variegation in favor of a green shape.

You can avoid some common problems by taking simple precautions. Minimize damage caused by heavy falls of snow on plants by knocking it off before it causes distortion and breakages. Protect container-grown topiary specimens, particularly at risk from frost damage to the roots, by wrapping insulation material (such as straw inside a plastic cover) around the container and over the top of the compost.

Established topiary in decline

The decline of established topiary is frequently the result of a deterioration in the growing conditions. Failure to feed plants over many years, particularly if combined with long periods of low rainfall and competition from weeds and grass, will result in poor, thin growth and, in the case of boxwood, the development of bare patches. Topiary will take new heart if you work a mulch of well-rotted organic matter into the soil around the base and apply a slow-release general fertilizer annually in early spring. The same applies to container-grown plants, which may need to be repotted in fresh compost in a larger container; the top layer of compost should be replenished annually. Deterioration of drainage and waterlogging on heavy soils is often responsible for poor growth or die-back. The causes may be heavy foot traffic over a long period or working around the topiary when the ground is wet. Spiking the ground may help but you may need to improve drainage more radically, for instance by installing a herringbone pattern of drains.

Topiary may suffer from competition with badly placed ornamentals encroaching on it. Letting in more light by removing overhead branches casting heavy shading will encourage growth. More radical solutions involve sacrificing plants or moving them, which you should stage over two or three years. In the fall of the first year or two, sever the lateral roots in a circle with a diameter of 40–48in (1–1.2m) around the trunk. With old specimens, cut half one year, the other half a year later. Move to a prepared position in the fall of the second or third year, wrapping the plant's root ball in burlap or plastic for the move.

Drastic measures

In some instances starting afresh may be the best course. Yew shows remarkable vigor, producing fresh growth even after drastic cutting back to the core, which allows a new shape to be built up from neglected yews. Cut back half the specimen in late spring of one year, the other half a year or two later, when plenty of fresh growth has been made. Boxwood will usually sprout from cut-back stems, but for both plants generous feeding, mulching with organic matter and watering in dry spells are essential. This high-level care should begin the year before renovation.

Well-cared-for topiary in yew and boxwood can be very long-lived. The garden at Levens Hall in Cumbria was laid out between 1689 and 1712, when the fashion for clipped evergreens was at its height in England. Almost all gardens of the period were swept away in the 18th century, when the new "natural" style of landscape gardening became the fashion. A stubborn though fortunate conservatism accounts for the survival of the garden's magnificent and bizarre collection of topiary.

PLANTS as ARCHITECTURE

Alcoves of dwarf boxwood contain a rich collection
of herbaceous and shrubby plants in a garden
divided by a battlemented yew hedge.

Formal hedges

Formal hedges, regular in outline and neatly trimmed, speak with authority, stating boldly where a boundary lies and making sharp demarcations within a given space. They control movement in the garden and direct the eye, in the process playfully concealing and then revealing views. They hide what is unsightly or simply dull and utilitarian, and make flattering backdrops or edgings to looser planting. Formal hedges exclude but also embrace, creating the most sheltered, intimate and secret corners of a garden. They are constant, a four-season framework for the garden, but are also ever-changing in the way that in their normal cycle of growth they reflect and absorb light, cast shadows and alter color. They give an impression of permanence and maturity. Although their effect of ordered calm is not achieved instantly, even a classic hedging plant such as yew will make a superb hedge more quickly than is generally expected and will require little more than one trim a year to maintain it in a state of architectural perfection.

Plants for formal hedges

Numerous plants are used for hedging in different parts of the world, choice being dictated by adaptability to climate and specific growing conditions such as exposure to strong, salt-laden sea winds. Nonetheless, the number of plants widely used throughout the temperate world for formal hedges is relatively small. These are valued because with regular trimming they develop a dense, well-finished surface and, having a slow to moderate rate of growth, they can be kept in shape with one or at most two trims a year. Boxwood and yew are the two most versatile evergreen hedging plants and are tolerant of a wide range of conditions. Boxwood, a broad-leaved evergreen with small leathery leaves, the upper surface dark green, can grow untrained to over 20ft (6m) and hedges of it almost 10ft (3m) high are known, although it is much more commonly seen clipped to a height of 5ft (1.5m) or less. For centuries the cultivar *Buxus sempervirens* 'Suffruticosa' has been

LEFT A firm low hedge of dwarf boxwood and the domed shapes of boxwood topiary contrast with the freer shapes and bright colors of an apparently casual mixture of plants. Flowering opium poppies and alstroemerias vie for attention with the jagged foliage of bearded irises and the rounded leaves of cabbages.

OPPOSITE Meticulous trimming underscores the assured lines of these straight and curved hedges, which impose order in a relaxed planting of shrubs and trees. The material used is privet, a fast-growing hedging plant that needs two or three trims a year.

OPPOSITE This garden, shown in late spring as the tulips are about to finish, uses a classic formula of generous planting that ensures a long succession of flowers within a permanent and ordered framework. An important component is an arbor running down the center of the garden, supporting climbing and rambling roses. The gravel paths are lined with granite paving blocks and the geometry of the layout is reinforced by low boxwood hedges.

RIGHT The contrasts of texture and color achieved when hedges of different plants are used in close proximity add depth and character to a garden. Here a dark yew hedge with a stepped top trimmed square is surrounded by a low hedge of cherry laurel, also with square top and vertical sides. Behind are stilt hedges of hornbeam, the blocks of foliage supported on gray trunks.

LEFT If left untrimmed the dwarf boxwood *Buxus sempervirens* 'Suffruticosa' can ultimately reach a height of 4ft (1.2m) or more. Here the plan is to use it as a formal edging to define a small bed, which has been thickly planted for a late spring display of the purplish black tulip 'Queen of Night.' A container of red lily-flowered tulips, supported so that the flowers stand above the deep maroon globes, adds a bright touch. The boxwood needs to be taken in hand when the tulips are over and would benefit from two trims in the summer.

used as an edging to flowerbeds, often kept to less than 12in (30cm) by regular clipping. Yew, a conifer with fine-textured dark green foliage, can make hedges of monumental scale; there is no more impressive though sober architecture to be made from plants.

Other broad-leaved evergreens used for hedging (covered in the Directory, page 148) include the hollies. The common or English holly (*Ilex aquifolium*) and the hybrid *I. × altaclerensis*, both of which have numerous plain-leaved and variegated cultivars, are

the most familiar; however, the American holly (*I. opaca*) comes into its own in its native eastern North America, where it is the hardiest broad-leaved evergreen tree. Hedging plants requiring three or more trims a year include the privets, of which the most widely planted (and unfairly maligned) is the semi-evergreen *Ligustrum ovalifolium*. An evergreen shrubby honeysuckle, *Lonicera nitida*, densely twiggy and small-leaved, is sometimes used as an alternative to boxwood for low hedges but requires up to five trims a year and is a greedy feeder. Portugal laurel and evergreen oak are also used.

The range of evergreen conifers suitable for hedges includes species of *Chamaecyparis*, *Cupressus*, *Juniperus*, *Thuja* and *Tsuga* (all covered in the Directory). Leyland cypress, which tolerates a wide range of conditions, including sea winds, and is fast-growing, has

ABOVE The billowing growth of foxgloves and other flowering plants is contained by a tall hornbeam hedge and a low hedge of dwarf boxwood, which is punctuated by cones to mark transitions in the garden. The planting in the beds is set back so that it does not flop over the low hedges.

EARLY TRAINING OF WIDELY USED HEDGING PLANTS

HORNBEAM
Other common hedging plants that are treated in the same way include beech.

A

B

C

1 Plant at 18–24in (45–60cm) intervals in the fall.
2 After planting, cut back the main stem and any long branches by one-third. (A)

3 In the fall or winter of the following year, cut back the main stem and branches by one-third again. (B)

4 In subsequent summers, trim the sides to the desired shape, cutting the upper surface level at the required height. (C)

BOXWOOD
Several common deciduous and semi-evergreen hedging plants, including hawthorn and privet, are treated in the same way, but need even more drastic cutting back at planting than boxwood. On planting they should be cut back to about 6in (15cm) above ground level, and in between fall and winter of the following year reduced by half.

A

B

C

1 Plant at 12–18in (30–45cm) intervals in early to mid-spring.
2 After planting, cut the main stems and laterals by about one-third. (A)

3 In spring of the following year, cut back all growths by about one-third.
4 In late summer of the following year, trim the sides lightly. (B)

5 In subsequent years, trim the sides to the required shape in early and late summer. (C)

YEW
Most conifers and many evergreens are best treated in the same way. The main stem is allowed to develop until the hedge has reached the desired height.

A

B

C

1 Plant at 20–24in (50–60cm) intervals in early to mid-spring, tying each plant to supports.
2 At planting, trim the plants lightly, cutting back thin growth. (A)

3 In late summer of the same year, trim the sides lightly. (B)
4 In early summer of the following year, remove the supports if the plants are firmly rooted.

5 In late summer, begin trimming the sides to the required shape.
6 In early and late summer of subsequent years, trim sides and top just below the hedge height. (C)

been very widely planted, but it is so vigorous it is better suited to use as an untrimmed windbreak.

Important deciduous hedging plants include hawthorn, the myrobalan or cherry plum (*Prunus cerasifera*) and, for low hedges, *Berberis thunbergii*, these last two being available as purple-leaved cultivars. However, their value is diminished by their annual loss of leaves. Clipped specimens of the European hornbeam and the European beech are exceptional in that they retain their foliage throughout winter and the change of color, warm brown in winter, adds seasonal drama to the garden.

Planting and early training

Deciduous trees or shrubs for hedging are commonly lifted from open ground in the dormant season and sold bare-root, with little or no soil adhering to them. Evergreens lifted in the dormant season are usually sold root-balled, with roots and soil wrapped in burlap or netting. Many evergreens and large specimens of deciduous trees and shrubs are sold container-grown. As a rule, the deciduous hedges are best planted in the fall in most places, evergreen hedges in early to mid-spring. Where winters are not severe—especially where mild moist winters are followed by hot dry summers, as in regions with a Mediterranean climate—fall planting is sensible for all hedges. In theory container-grown trees and shrubs can be planted at any time of the year, but without conscientious watering there are likely to be losses from summer plantings. To make a satisfactory formal hedge the plants need to be uniform in growth and coloring; there is such variation in boxwood and yew, for example, that uniformity can be guaranteed only if plants are from the same clone. For this reason it is worth getting stock from a reputable supplier and ordering a few extra to plant separately as reserves, to fill gaps if there are failures.

It may be tempting to use plants that have already made considerable growth, as they seem to offer the best chance of achieving a mature hedge quickly. However, the cost is high and the results are almost always disappointing; even if such plants do not fail they are often slow to get established. Vigorous young plants are a much better buy: they often overtake older plants and ultimately produce a stronger and denser hedge.

With most of the standard plants, you can make a solid hedge in a single line and by ranging the plants 12–24in (30–60cm) apart. For conifers the normal planting distance is about 24in (60cm); for deciduous trees such as beech and hornbeam 18in (45cm); for most shrubs, including boxwood, about 12in (30cm), but for dwarf hedging, including *Buxus sempervirens* 'Suffruticosa,' 4–6in (10–15cm). In the past, hedges were sometimes planted as staggered double rows to gain width but the practice is not advisable: such hedges invariably become gappy and bare at the base. The design will dictate the choice of plant and the height of a hedge. When planning a tall hedge it is important to calculate the area it will shade when fully developed and the maintenance problems that it may create. A space between the bed or border and the hedge is essential for easy trimming. Setting up ladders and trestles or adjustable platforms (easier to work from than ladders) requires time and a reasonable level of fitness and agility.

To provide good conditions for the unnaturally close permanent planting of a hedge, you need to prepare the ground well. The ideal is to double-dig a trench 24–36in (60–90cm) wide along the planting line, breaking up the subsoil and incorporating copious quantities of well-rotted organic matter. Plants need to be well firmed in and set at the same depth they have been growing at in the nursery. Deeper planting is often the cause of failures, especially with yew hedges. If the position is exposed, the hedge should be sheltered by a screen of netting or burlap. Loss of moisture in cold, drying winds is often the cause of failure among broad-leaved and coniferous evergreens. Conifers benefit from light staking with bamboo canes until the roots get established.

A sound hedge is clothed to the ground in foliage. Early pruning (see page 85) aims to encourage growth low down. Many successful hedges have vertical sides but tapering the hedge, often producing a pleasing visual effect of stability, helps to maintain a full bottom and reduces the labor of trimming. A suitable batter is 2–4in (5–10cm) for every 12in (30cm) of height. The batter, as the taper is known, allows more light to reach the base of the hedge and reduces the effect of apical dominance, which suppresses lower growth. It also helps to deflect strong winds, and a narrow top to a hedge minimizes the potential damage from accumulations of snow.

Maintaining formal hedges

A formal hedge is nothing unless trimmed regularly. The ultimate structure of the hedge is the old growth, the stratum to which every trim returns. Clipping regimes vary to some extent according to the plant (see the Directory, page 148). It is difficult to maintain the lines and angles of a formal hedge without the use of guides. You can mark horizontals at the top and bottom with garden line stretched tight between upright stakes and checked against a spirit level. A template is useful if a precise angle is to be maintained over broken lengths of hedging. It is often assumed that a hedge does not need feeding, but the plants of a hedge face stiff competition from each other for the available nutrients in the soil, so you need to apply a balanced general fertilizer annually in spring and eliminate competition from weeds. Hedges also rob neighboring beds and borders of nutrients. Boxwood, for example, forms a mat of roots extending laterally from a hedge. You can control their spread by cutting through them with a spade about 4in (10cm) from either side of the hedge every two or three years.

An armillary sphere forms the centerpiece of a garden compartment, where a coating of hoarfrost highlights the severe geometry of hedges and topiary in yew and boxwood, with horizontals and matched shapes scrupulously maintained.

Ornamented and informal hedges

Although a basic hedge, a straightforward assertion of verticals and horizontals in a uniform color, helps create an air of tranquil stability, sometimes, if for instance no plants or built features rise above it, its unrelieved horizontals and unvarying color can seem excessive. But a formal hedge, like good architecture, can take a degree of ornamentation, provided the sense of a fundamentally stable order is not undermined, while an informal hedge, looser in shape, often carries a seasonal decoration of flowers and fruits.

Mixed hedges

Consistent color and texture are among the conventional virtues of the formal hedge. As explained earlier, the best chance of achieving these is to plant with the same clone for the whole length of a hedge (see page 86). But variation, too, can be pleasing, as chance mixtures show, and a hedge deliberately composed of different plants can have great ornamental value. The boldness of tapestry or marbled effects depends on the character of the plants grown together. At one extreme is the laid farm hedge: this has a kind of yeoman formality when periodically cut back and branches, nearly severed and bent down, are woven between uprights. But its trees and shrubs develop into a complex mixture, which may support climbers and shelter annuals, perennials and bulbs. At the other is a hedge composed of mixed seedlings of a single species, the result being subtle differences of shade and texture, often showing most distinctly when the hedge is side-lit. Mixtures of different cultivars with distinctive leaf color make stronger contrasts. A much used bold combination is a plain-leaved beech and a purple-leaved form, such as *Fagus sylvatica* 'Riversii.' Almost

LEFT Mixed textures and colors of yew, privet and beeches, plain- and purple-leaved, make an attractive detail, although limiting the mixture to two plants would make the hedge easier to maintain and create a more pleasing overall impression.

OPPOSITE Sloping buttresses in yew run back from a low boxwood hedge to a brick wall, forming a series of compartments, which have been planted with a collection of roses. To make convincing green architecture the buttresses must be clipped at a consistent angle.

as striking are mixtures of plain- and yellow-leaved cultivars of yew or of plain and variegated hollies. Different species such as yew and holly growing together also create strong contrasts.

The best way of creating a deliberate tapestry effect is to mix together plants that have a similar rate of growth and tolerate the same clipping regime. Differences in vigor usually mean that one plant or cultivar is more dominant than another. As a rule variegated cultivars of a plant grow at a slower rate than plain-leaved cultivars. One way of dealing with these differences is to use one kind of plant for the main run of a hedge and another only for buttresses (see page 91). The tapestry effect of plants growing through each other is sacrificed but the contrasts stand out.

A plain seat of wooden slats has been transformed into a charming garden bench by a back and buttress-like armrests in boxwood. The back has been clipped in elegant curves. The armrests, one C-shaped, the other a C-shape reversed, are trimmed from boxwood plants growing in containers at each end of the seat. Although the bench invites loungers to take their ease, the boxwood parts of it are intended as visual effects, not as real supports.

Varying the line of a hedge

The designs in which hedges feature as major components are predominantly rectilinear: hedges mark the square boundaries and axes run at right angles to one another. However, the serpentine hedge, though requiring many more plants than a straight hedge and more time to trim, looks and is wonderfully extravagant. Curved hedges are often useful in small to medium-size gardens, where their embracing movement helps to create an intimate environment while blocking out unwanted views (as in the garden illustrated on page 109). You need to measure and mark out carefully the lines of serpentine and curved hedges before planting.

Adjusting the width is a more common way of altering the line of a hedge. A buttress in masonry or brickwork projecting from a wall gives additional strength, or the illusion of it. Trimmed living buttresses projecting from a hedge give no significant support but convey an impression of architectural solidity. A buttress at the end of a hedge helps to anchor it. A pair can flank an opening, giving the opening importance, or be used to create a frame for a container or a piece of sculpture (as in the garden illustrated on page 109). The projection of a buttress casts a shadow and a succession of buttresses along the line of a hedge, although they may be no more than shallow rectangular pilasters, create rhythmic contrasts of light and shade, more or less dramatic according to the position of the sun. When extended well beyond the sides of a hedge, buttresses form bays, making attractive compartments for flowers. In a long border buttresses make a flattering background to flowers in summer and become a dominant ornamental feature between fall and spring. Although normally planted to project from a hedge, living buttresses can also serve as visual supports to brick and masonry walls.

A hedge and its buttresses are usually of the same plant material. You do not need to plant outside the line of the hedge to create small buttresses; merely establishing the necessary projection in the early stages of shaping is enough. However, you will need to plant additional, subsidiary hedges at right angles to the main hedge if the buttresses are to extend far enough to form bays. Doubling up of planting may be necessary for a massive effect, typically at the ends of a hedge, and to create adequate bulk in low hedges, for example dwarf boxwood. In such cases replace one or two plants in the row with a pair or pairs, setting the plants on each side of the main line of the hedge. For a contrasted effect, you could use one kind of plant for the hedge and another for the buttresses, but before planting it is worth thinking through the impact this will make on the mature garden; the ornamental value of contrasts may be less important than the unifying effect of hedges and buttresses of the same material.

Happy proportions and an attractive shape are essential. A buttress can be simply a vertical pier or pillar, half to two-thirds the height of the hedge, with its top sloping upward into the hedge. A cube, topped by a ball or cone, makes a strong terminus. You could follow architectural models for more elaborate designs, perhaps with the extremity marked by a finial (see page 96). But avoid fussiness: a fussy shape will take away from the overall design of a garden and maintenance will be difficult.

Another way of modifying the line of a hedge is to cut shallow recesses into it, for instance to accommodate sculpture. A simple niche without framing buttresses can produce a pleasingly subdued effect; the device was much used in the past to create the impression of a garden haunted by mythological figures, the busts or statues just set back into the hedge. Deeper recesses produce stronger contrasts of light and shade and are capable of accommodating large-scale sculpture or seating; it is best to plan them from the outset, moving the line of the hedge back on a curve or at right angles to form the recess.

Arches and windows

Hedge screens and openings in them transform the garden into theater, especially when combined with changes of level. The arch is the perfect device for framing an opening and the view it affords, whether it is a tantalizing glimpse or a prospect revealed in all its detail. An arch also gives weight to the axis on which it lies and a hierarchy of arches can help to impose order on the garden. Like a niche, an arch can frame a piece of statuary or even a planted container, the view behind providing a backdrop.

You can make an arch of any hedging plant that grows to 10ft (3m) or more. An arch is particularly effective in the dark green

TRAINING A BEECH HEDGE WITH AN ARCH OVER AN OPENING

A

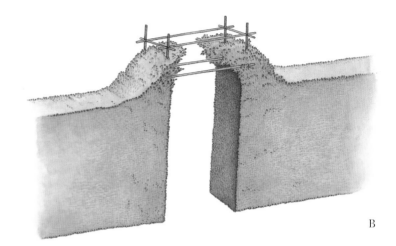

B

The aim is to train an arch over an opening 4ft (1.2m) wide in a beech hedge 6ft (1.8m) high.

MATERIALS REQUIRED

Sufficient young beech trees (*Fagus sylvatica*) for the required length of hedge to plant at average intervals of 18in (45cm)

4 strong wooden stakes 10–12ft (3–3.7m) long

4 bamboo canes of good thickness over 6ft (1.8m) long, and 4 bamboo canes about 14in (35cm) long

Strong cord and tarred string

Shears; hand pruners

1 Begin by following the first three steps in the instructions for the training of a hornbeam hedge (see page 85). The hedge needs to be planted with a gap of about 5½ft (1.6m) between the plants where the opening is to be.
2 In the summer of the second and subsequent years after planting, trim the sides and, when the hedge is 6ft (1.8m) high, insert a pair of vertical stakes on each side of the gap to serve as supports for the developing arch. They must be well secured and stand about 8ft (2.5m) high.

The pairs of stakes should be about 5ft (1.5m) apart, and the distance between the stakes in each pair 8–10in (20–25cm). The pairs should be fixed to one another by parallel horizontal bamboo canes, four tied at a height of 6½ft (2m) and four at 7½ft (2.3m). (A)
3 When the beech hedge has reached a height of 6ft (1.8m), trim the upper surface level except for about 32in (80cm) on each side of the opening.
4 In the summer of subsequent years, trim the

and precise architecture of yew. An extended arch becomes a tunnel, particularly dark and mysterious in yew. The simplest kind of arch is formed by a plain opening in a tall hedge, with the solid mass of the hedge closing over the top of the opening. An extravagant use of this kind of arch is the arcade: solid hedge supported by hedge piers standing above a sequence of openings. Even more monumental is an arch in a block of hedge that is taller and wider than the hedge extending on each side of it. The most common arch is a frame over an opening in a hedge where the top of the frame is higher than the hedge on each side. The similarities between these various kinds of arch are greater than their differences and in broad terms all are formed along the lines described above for an arch in beech. Initially, you train the growths

that form the arch on supports from both sides to meet at the center, and remove the supports when the branches have knitted together and are self-supporting. Although a narrow arch can be cut square, an arch in which the growths are pulled across on a curve is easier to train, and stronger. A wide arch is slow to train and, without supports, particularly vulnerable to damage by snow and strong winds. A good average span for an arch in a hedge is 4ft (1.2m), and a height of 6½–7ft (2–2.2m) at the midpoint of the arch gives adequate clearance. To be architecturally convincing the crown of the arch must have a certain weight. If it is less than about 12in (30cm) thick, it will look flimsy. With a monumental arch in a thick hedge the problem is shade, some areas within the arch getting insufficient light to make good growth.

C

rest of the hedge but allow the growths on each side of the gap to grow vertically and train branches to form an arch, tying them with tarred string to the horizontals between the upright stakes. (B)

5 When the arch is well formed, remove the upright stakes and bamboo canes, if necessary continuing to tie branches to one another until the arch is complete.

6 Trim the completed arch at the same time as clipping the rest of the hedge. (C)

You can cut an opening in an existing hedge by removing two or three plants; this is a radical approach that allows an established garden to be rearranged with a different layout and axes. If the hedge is old it may take some time to train growths across the top and for the sides of the arch to become leafy. On the principle that pruning stimulates growth, some cutting back at the top of the span will speed up the development of growths to complete the top of the hedge.

Cutting openings is also a way to create windows in an existing hedge. Where shelter and privacy are key considerations, and the only view to expose is dull or ugly, this is not a step to take lightly. But where an existing hedge creates a claustrophobic atmosphere, opening windows in it can make the garden seem lighter and more

Screens and openings in a garden control the way visitors experience it. An arch through a hornbeam hedge frames a view into a compartment laid out formally with low boxwood hedging and paired yuccas in urns.

Curved and stepped silhouettes

Finials rising above the hedge line (see page 96) are a light and elegant way of breaking the horizontal. Two more fundamental approaches involve cutting the top of the hedge in steps or giving it a curved outline. A central section one step above the main level of the hedge makes a simple design that can be added to, perhaps with stepped sections at either end. A crenelated silhouette is made up of repeated steps of the same height, the battlements creating a rhythmically broken line with dramatic contrasts of light and shade. A hedge with its top edge making a concave curving line dipping between high points seems to be suspended from two or a series of piers. Curves springing up from piers or at regular intervals along the horizontal create an arched outline. Curves at the ends of a hedge can be elaborated into scrolls. A pretty backing to a garden seat consists of a hedge whose outline is arched at the center and subsides into gentler curves on each side. At the end of a hedge, or at each side of an opening, a scalloped curve or a curving buttress make elegant finishes. Even established hedges can sometimes be reshaped with curves and steps; vigorous and healthy yew and boxwood usually respond well when cut back (see page 127).

The many variations that can be played on these themes are easily developed from the basic hedge, but precision in the planning and cutting are essential for the ornamentation to be effective. A plan of the hedge drawn to scale is invaluable as a guide at the outset and as a point of reference until the hedge is fully formed. You can achieve a successful silhouette only with unhurried and carefully measured trimming at the early stages. It is helpful to mark out with stakes key linear measurements such as end points of a step, the centerpoint of an arch, points where an arch meets the level surface of a hedge and apertures in battlements. The key line, above and below which there is variation, should be horizontal for hedges on level ground; when any trimming is done it should be marked first with taut garden line checked against a spirit level. In the case of a hedge trimmed to follow a slope, the key line, which you can establish with measured stakes, runs parallel to the ground. In the formative stages vertical growth above the basic hedge line must be left to develop to make curved extensions and steps. Light

airy. And from the privileged position of a hedge window, as from a picture window in a Chinese pavilion, a framed view over a landscape or into another compartment of a garden gives a frisson of delight. The spacing of the constituent plants of a hedge usually dictates where it will be easy to create windows. It is sometimes possible to make an opening less than 24in (60cm) across between main stems, but for a more generous window you will need to cut at least one plant at the desired height and then train growths across on bamboo canes or twine, as if completing an arch. It is, of course, better to plan windows from the outset, spacing hedge plants appropriately, making cuts when the bottom line of the window has been reached and completing the hedge wall when plants are still making vigorous growth. A metal frame supported at ground level and incorporated when the hedge is planted provides a training guide and gives a firm definition to the window.

ABOVE Compartments within compartments are defined by different kinds of hedging. Beech hedges surround two enclosures; within these, low boxwood hedges outline beds planted with perennials. Arches in the beech are positioned on the central axis, mirroring one another. Their curved tops are matched by the curved hedge corners, where right angles would be more usual.

OPPOSITE The best use of windows in hedges is when they offer unexpected views. They can reveal a prospect beyond the garden, in the way Japanese gardens take in borrowed landscapes; allow parts of a garden to be seen from unusual vantage points; or frame a piece of sculpture or topiary shape. There is something unsettling about this peephole giving a view of a seat where the unwitting sitter might expect privacy. A metal frame, inserted as the beech hedge develops, frames the window.

pruning to form a downward curve can begin before the hedge has grown to the maximum height required. Using a template—made of plywood and attached to a stake, and in the shape of the curve to be repeated—can simplify the trimming of small-scale repeated curves, such as arches above or bites into the horizontal. Before using it as a guide, make sure that the measurements and shape fit the length of the hedge, by placing it in a succession of measured positions and checking its top against a horizontal garden line. Templates are usually too cumbersome for large-scale shapes.

With a mature hedge the old growth provides the trimming guide but even so lines are invaluable for marking the key horizontal, the low point of downward curves and the top point of crenelations and arches. A measuring rod cut to size is useful when the same measure is repeated many times, as, for example, in the case of battlements.

TRAINING A YEW BUTTRESS WITH A TULIP FINIAL

To train a finial as part of a buttress or hedge, you should space plants so that a leader is available to train up as the finial. The buttress illustrated projects 6½ft (2m) from a main hedge and is planted with four yews.

MATERIALS REQUIRED
Four vigorous young yew trees (*Taxus baccata*) 30–40in (75–100cm) high
Shears; hand pruners

A

1 For the initial training of the yew, follow steps 1 to 5 on page 85. The four yews should be fairly closely and evenly spaced, the outermost about 12in (30cm) in from the end of the buttress. (A)
2 When the buttress has reached a height of 40in (1m), in summer trim the sides and the upper surface where growths are not required for the vertical extension of the buttress and finial. (B)

B

C

3 In the following and subsequent summers, shape the curve of the buttress and the tulip shape of the finial, cutting back the leaders only when they are slightly taller than the required height. Keep the leader of the finial growing until it is just over 6½ft (2m); then cut it back by about 6in (15cm) to shape the ball. (C)

D

4 When the tulip shape and ball are fully formed, trim at the same time as the rest of the buttress. (D)

Finials and hedge-top topiary
The finial, an architectural ornament capping a distinctive feature, transfers readily to green architecture composed of plants that can be clipped into tight shapes. It has been widely used in the past, particularly on evergreen hedges in yew, boxwood and holly. A characteristic example is the use of ball finials topping buttresses standing at each side of an opening in a hedge, the accent serving to underline an important transition in the garden. Simple symmetrical shapes from the standard topiary repertoire are the most commonly used, but there is a place, too, for various vase and urn shapes, and stylized versions of beasts and birds. Heraldic eagles and lions or chess knights might make suitably imposing finials at the main gate to a large house. Whatever the shape, it will

work as an ornament only if it is in proportion to the feature it decorates. Rhythmic repetition can be a unifying device in the garden, as, for example, when each buttress of a sequence in parallel ends in a trained shape, either identical or variations on a theme. An evenly spaced row of finials can make an intriguing frieze to a garden, casting a shadow as fascinating as the outline. It is a matter of judgment as to when ornamentation on this scale becomes overpowering or neurotically fussy.

The finial is an appropriate ornament for gardens of regular layout. Another kind of hedge-top topiary, usually consisting of stylized animals and birds, is much freer in spirit and is suitable for a wide variety of gardens. Isolated creatures, bold in silhouette, strut and preen or small groups—hens and rooster, cat and

kittens, hounds and fleeing fox—are frozen in green tableaux.

The techniques for training finials and other hedge-top topiary are the same as for other topiary shapes. The essential requirement is a strong stem left to grow above the height of the hedge. Shape side growths as required and cut back the stem itself only to complete the shape. For a regular layout there must be plants well placed so that their vertical leaders can be developed into finials in the required positions. You may need several stems for more fanciful hedge-top topiary, for example to form the legs of an animal. Shape these by tying growths together or to supports, firmly anchored in the hedge. The knots of the ties, made with tarred string, must not be so tight that they constrict growth. Bamboo canes are suitable for training simple shapes and can be removed when the shape is complete. Wire frames, which give more detail, are difficult to dismantle without damaging the finished shape and are generally best left in position, although they may cause rubbing. You can carefully trim the finished shape at the same time as the hedge or even more frequently to preserve its lines.

ABOVE At Nymans in West Sussex, England, a thick yew hedge is topped by a magnificent array of pyramid finials. There is nice detailing in the curves at the base of the finials. What makes maintaining a hedge of this scale and finish time-consuming is that levels and angles must be carefully checked and much of the work has to be done above ground on platforms, moved as work proceeds.

LEFT The combination of curves and crenelations gives this hedge an impressive silhouette. The thickness of the hedge presents a greater problem for management than the trimming of the shapes.

OPPOSITE ABOVE Boxwood is on the whole so slow-growing that mophead standards on such sturdy stems rising out of a low hedge are truly impressive. Boxwood standards of this scale are best trained from a vigorous cultivar such as *Buxus sempervirens* 'Handsworthiensis.'

OPPOSITE BELOW In parts of Europe topiary standards, often of holly, are still sometimes preserved as components of farm hedges. Here the idea has been translated to the garden boundary. Dome-shaped finials rise from a hornbeam hedge flanking a simple gate, which marks a transition from the wildest reaches of the garden to farmland and woodland.

Informal hedges

The dense uniform surfaces of a formal hedge hide the constituent plants, which are totally subordinated to the architecture of the whole. But with an informal hedge shears do not have the same absolute authority. The barrier such a hedge makes is clearly composed of individual plants ranged in line, although not separated as they would be in an avenue. Some trimming maintains a loose overall shape but it is geared to the plant's natural growth and encourages impressive displays of flowers and fruit.

Although there are considerable aesthetic differences between formal and informal hedges, the two types can be useful in similar ways. Informal hedges too can be used to mark the boundaries of a garden and create divisions within it. Aromatic plants such as hyssop (*Hyssopus officinalis*), lavender (*Lavandula angustifolia*), rosemary (*Rosmarinus officinalis*) and cotton lavender (*Santolina chamaecyparissus*), whether lightly or more severely trimmed, are perennially popular as edging. Private and secluded areas can be created inside a framework of informal hedges. Provided they are high and thick enough, these hedges are particularly effective at filtering wind and creating sheltered areas—often better for this purpose than formal hedges, which can be so dense that they create almost as much turbulence as solid walls. As backgrounds and foregrounds to other plantings, informal hedges contrast less sharply than formal hedges with the flowing lines and colorful displays of beds and borders, their own flowers and fruit often forming part of a general display.

Plants for informal hedges

The range of plants grown as informal hedges in all climatic regions is very large. Almost all are of naturally dense growth and some of the most popular plants are those that carry a profusion of flower or berries over a long season, light pruning allowing the buds to develop. In tropical and subtropical gardens, plants such as the Chinese hibiscus (*Hibiscus rosa-sinensis*) flower almost all year round. Even in temperate gardens there are informal hedge plants with long flowering seasons, among them escallonias, *Fuchsia magellanica*, Japanese quince (*Chaenomeles*), and numerous Shrub and Bush roses. *Berberis* x *stenophylla*, forsythias, mock oranges

(*Philadelphus coronarius*) and many others flower profusely but over a shorter season. Among the most showy fruits are the tomato-like hips of the rugosa roses but several berrying shrubs give a longer display. The red fruits of *Cotoneaster lacteus* and the white of the snowberries (*Symphoricarpos*) are conspicuous right into winter.

Some hedge plants are chosen because their spiny or thorny growth makes impenetrable barriers. The hawthorns (*Crataegus*) have been much used as traditional field boundaries, sometimes as constituents of a mixed hedge that is drastically cut back on a regular cycle, the partly cut stems being laid almost horizontally (see page 88). Other thorny and spiky plants include the Japanese bitter orange (*Poncirus trifoliata*), and, in arid conditions, the prickly pear (*Opuntia*) and other cacti. The bamboos (*Fargesia*) are among the most graceful of all the screening plants but many spread rampantly. *F. murieliae* and *F. nitida* are outstandingly beautiful, with slender canes bowing gracefully under a billowing mass of elegant foliage, and neither spreads uncontrollably. Plants tolerant of sea gales laden with salt spray that can be grown as informal hedges are of enormous value in coastal gardens, where they provide a sheltered and protected environment for more vulnerable plants. The broadleaf (*Griselinia littoralis*) makes a dense hedge of lustrous apple-green leaves but its flowers are inconspicuous. Escallonias, *Fuchsia magellanica* and tamarisk (*Tamarix ramosissima*) all make flowering hedges that will tolerate rigorous coastal conditions. A fuller selection of plants suitable for informal hedges in temperate regions is given on page 154.

Planting, training and maintenance

As with formal hedges (see page 80), the ground needs to be well prepared before planting and the row marked out with a line. Planting distances depend on the plant but most shrubs that grow to 3ft (90cm) high need to be planted 20–24in (50–60cm) apart, shorter-growing plants 10–20in (25–50cm). Most need little more than light trimming at planting to encourage their natural bushiness.

Apart from the standard routine of removing dead, diseased and damaged wood, many informal hedges require little regular pruning. Minor adjustments only are needed for compact plants such as *Berberis thunbergii* 'Bagatelle,' or the erect rosemary *Rosmarinus officinalis* 'Miss Jessopp's Upright.' Other informal hedges benefit more from systematic pruning than clipping; the regime is usually slightly more severe than would be appropriate for the plant if it were growing in the open garden. As a general rule, prune shrubs that flower in spring, such as forsythias, immediately after flowering to maintain the hedge's general shape and to encourage the development of young growths, which in most cases bear flowers more freely than old wood. Prune shrubs that flower in mid- to late summer on new wood produced during the growing season in late winter to early spring. You can follow this regime with roses, which perform best if stems are trimmed back annually and some old wood removed at the same time. Lavender hedges, too, are best trimmed annually in spring to prevent bushes from becoming leggy. The effect of newly trimmed lavender is almost as regular as topiary or a formal hedge.

Several plants most commonly seen as informal hedges can also be trimmed to a more regular shape. Forsythias and escallonias are two examples. The more severe clipping needed, which may have to be carried out two or three times a year, reduces the amount of flowers produced, but in these two cases the floral display can still be impressive.

Chaenomeles speciosa 'Cardinalis' and other Japanese quinces often begin to bear their saucer-shaped flowers in mid-winter. They are deciduous shrubs of tangled growth that can be trained against walls or clipped to form low informal hedges. The best time to trim them is immediately after flowering so that the following year's display is not seriously reduced.

Pleached and pollarded trees

A screen of foliage raised above ground level is useful for blocking out unsightly views and can create shelter and privacy without enclosing areas of the garden claustrophobically. Unlike dense hedges, raised screens also allow cold air to drain away. They can be made from climbers on supports, but there is a long practice of training trees for this purpose and you can apply the techniques creatively even on a small scale.

Pleached screens

Pleaching is a method of training trees with flexible branches, particularly species of linden (*Tilia*), which are interwoven to form a screen. It is most commonly used to train plants into a vertical screen, the growths being trained out to left and right of main stems trimmed clean to a height of about 6½ft (2m). As well as having flexible shoots, lindens have attractive leaves and fragrant flowers; but when choosing the species to plant, you should also consider their drawbacks. Common or European linden (*T.* x *europaea*), although widely planted, produces numerous suckers at the base, which spoil the effect of an avenue and may interfere with other planting. It is also prone to aphid attack and unsightly sooty mold develops on the sticky honeydew excreted by the aphids. *T.* x *euchlora*, which has glossy leaves, does not sucker and is free from aphids; its flowers, however, tend to make bees drowsy, so it is not suitable to plant where children are likely to play, and there have been disease problems with it. The red-twigged linden (*T. platyphyllos* 'Rubra') is not resistant to aphid attack but produces fewer suckers than the common linden and has a good health record. Its red-brown young shoots are attractive in winter.

LEFT The dense growth common hornbeam produces in response to trimming has made it the most widely planted deciduous tree in Europe for formal hedges. The gray trunks make a sturdy support when it is trained as a pleached stilt hedge.

OPPOSITE The pliant shoots of linden trees make them well suited for training as aerial hedges. Here lindens are being trained in two concentric circles to create a shady walk.

PLEACHING A LINDEN AVENUE TO FORM AN AERIAL SCREEN

Avenues of pleached linden on clear stems are most commonly seen as features in large gardens, but it is possible to train a short screen that will fit into a smaller garden. Various support systems are used to ensure vertical growth of the main stem and to support the horizontal arms, and some support is often retained even when the screen is mature. The screen can be strengthened by side-grafting the horizontally trained stems of neighboring trees.

MATERIALS REQUIRED

Support system in place on well-prepared ground, consisting of the following: two guyed posts 12ft (3.7m) high and 33ft (10m) apart and a metal upright of the same height halfway between; four strained horizontal wires, the lowest at a height of 6½ft (2m), the topmost at 10ft (3m) and the remaining two spaced evenly between them

4 matched specimens of lime (*Tilia platyphyllos* 'Rubra'), 6½–8ft (2–2.5m) high and with young laterals

4 bamboo canes, 4 of 10ft (3m) and 4 of 40in (1m)

Tree ties; tarred string

Hand pruners and loppers

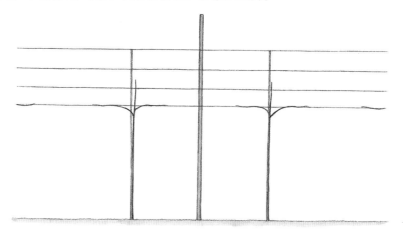

A

1 In late fall or early winter, plant the young trees all on the same side of the support system and spaced 8ft (2.5m) apart, starting 4ft (1.2m) from the end posts. If the plants are tall enough, orient them in such a way that the maximum number of laterals can be trained out parallel to the framework.

2 For each tree, insert a bamboo cane into the ground, on the other side, hard against the wires, and secure the trees to their canes.

3 Tie in any branches that can be trained left and right along the wires. Cut out any laterals above the wire that cannot be tied in. (A)

Pleached linden screens, normally planted as described above, are sometimes planted to create a garden authentic to a particular period but are valuable in the garden for more than their historical interest. They create a lighter and less static effect than many hedge screens, partly because of the free-fluttering movement of the leaves; they form strongly defined avenues, and bulbs and perennials can be planted beneath. As, unlike dense hedges and walls, they allow cold air to drain away, they do not create frost pockets or cause wind turbulence. And although pleached lindens are most commonly seen as aerial screens, the horizontal training can begin just above ground level; or the aerial screen can be combined with a lower formal hedge below, planted parallel to it—useful if privacy is important. Once established, a pleached screen does not require a lot of maintenance. If the screen is high, the work is more easily done from a platform than from a ladder.

Stilt hedges

A more typical hedge shape is produced when hornbeam is trained up on stems and pleached. When clipped, hornbeam produces densely twiggy growth and is therefore better trained to make what are sometimes called aerial or stilt hedges. The framework necessary to support a conventional hedge shape in its formative stage usually consists of strongly braced end posts carrying several rows of wires at heights of 6ft (1.8m), 9ft (2.7m) and 12ft (3.7m). It is erected over the line of the projected hedge before it is planted. The central leader of each plant is trained up but the lower branches are retained until the trunk has started to thicken up, usually by the time the leader has reached the second level of wires. Once the leader has reached the bottom wires, a combination of winter pruning and tying in eventually produces a hedge shape. Remove the framework when the hedge is well formed.

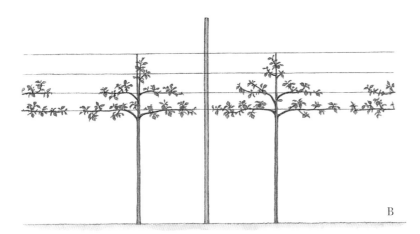

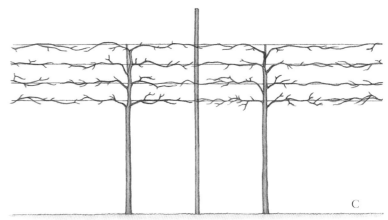

4 During the same summer, tie in the leader vertically as it develops and all new branches that can be trained left and right to the framework of wires, cutting off or pinching out growths that grow out from the face of the screen. (B)
5 In winter of the same year, remove shoots growing out from the face of the screen, and cut long laterals above the bottom wire back to two or three buds.

6 In subsequent years, continue a program of summer and winter pruning and training, weaving and tying the branches of adjacent trees together. When the leader is tall enough, train it along the top wire in one direction and a branch in the other to form the top tier. (C)

MAINTAINING A PLEACHED SCREEN
The main pruning and training is carried out in winter but loose growths can also be tied in or woven with other branches in the second half of summer. Cut out growths that cannot be trained in, and cut back to a bud all shoots that extend beyond the outline of the screen. Rub off any shoots that develop on the trunks of trees below the bottom tier and cut off suckers growing at the base.

Tunnels and arbors

Tunnels made from pleached trees are faster-growing and make a much lighter effect than monumental and darkly mysterious hedge tunnels in yew and other evergreens. You can also use pleaching to create the shade for arbors and bowers, although climbers trained on trellis are often better suited to seating areas on a relatively small scale. Hornbeam and linden, the standard trees for making pleached tunnels and arbors, need to be trained on a permanent framework. In the past, wooden frameworks of various kinds were used; in the modern garden sturdy metal arches with wires at regular intervals provide a more practical support. A suitable framework for a hornbeam tunnel over a path 6–8ft (1.8–2.5m) wide would be 7–8ft (2.2–2.5m) high at the center, with metal arches at intervals of about 4ft (1.2m) and with a minimum number of five horizontal metal ties, at 30in (75cm) and 5ft (1.5m) on each

side, and down the center. In addition to these, it is necessary to have a grid of wires spaced about 10in (25cm) apart, to which growths can be tied. In the fall plant matched specimens that have already produced a few laterals on each side of the supports. The aim of formative training is to take leaders up from each side to the center of the arch while at the same time encouraging the growth of laterals, which are trained out to left and right. Remove shoots that grow into or away from the frame. Winter pruning maintains a dense, even cover without growths overlapping.

You can play a number of variations on this theme, for example with closer planting or by training the hornbeams with clear stems to a height of about 6ft (1.8m) and growing along the base at each side of the arch a dense hedge, say of yew, to a height of about 4½ft (1.4m). A windowed tunnel of this kind makes a refreshingly shaded walk from which to view contrasting compartments of a

OPPOSITE A covered avenue, bare in winter and early spring but deliciously shady in the heat of summer, consists of London planes (*Platanus × hispanica*) trained up on clear stems to a height of about 10ft (3m), their horizontal growth restricted to inward-growing arms that meet to form a canopy.

BELOW Pleached lindens are usually trained so that the foliage surface makes a vertical screen. Another option is to train the branches out horizontally at a fixed height above ground level so as to create a cool shaded area for the summer months. In this garden a single linden has been trained like an extended standard, the trunk clear to a height of about 8ft (2.5m), above which branches are spaced out on a support system.

garden. A few flowering trees also lend themselves to pleaching. Laburnum, damned as epitomizing suburbia, can be triumphantly successful grown on a support—especially *Laburnum × watereri* 'Vossii,' whose trailing yellow racemes are particularly long.

Pollarded trees

Pollarding is a traditional method of woodland management that is sometimes applied to ornamental trees. A tree is trained up on a single stem and the branches forming the head cut back on a regular basis. Formerly, in the case of trees of economic importance the pruning cycle ensured the production of poles that could be harvested for timber or firewood. The cuts were usually made at a height of 6ft (1.8m) or more so that the new growth could not be browsed by cattle. Pollarding and the similar technique of coppicing, in which shrubs and trees are cut back near to the base, are applied to some ornamentals. For example, several species of willow (*Salix*) are hard-pruned to keep up the production of young stems, as these are more colorful than mature wood. These techiques are also used to encourage the growth of large ornamental leaves, particularly of plants such as the purple-leaved hazel (*Corylus maxima* 'Purpurea').

Pollarding is also used to maintain street and garden trees at a fixed height, the branches being cut back to short stumps, sometimes over 6½ft (2m) long, every two or three years. The London plane (*Platanus × hispanica* syn. *P. × acerifolia*), favored as a city tree because it withstands atmospheric pollution, is remarkably tolerant of this severe regime. Several branches may be trained out and then regularly cut back to the same point. If training keeps growth to two planes the pollarded tree creates a screen of foliage in summer. Less ornamental is the mute protest of the grotesquely swollen and distorted stubs that are revealed in winter. It is therefore in general better to choose another method of creating a screen, perhaps using a trained climber for quickest results. If you are taking over a garden where trees have been pollarded, the best course is to maintain the pruning regime, by cutting back, preferably in the fall. Long branches that are allowed to develop from the pollarded stumps may present a hazard as, usually, they are not strongly attached.

Counterpoint of hedges and topiary

Hedges and topiary are key elements in this rectangular country garden, approximately 65ft (20m) by 100ft (30m), where they create divisions and connections between a number of different compartments. These in themselves can serve as models for smaller gardens. An angle of rendered wall shelters the pool but a glittering hedge of the common or English holly (*Ilex aquifolium*) marks most of the rest of the boundary; the polished leaves of the cultivar 'J.C. van Tol' have the advantage of being almost spineless. The layout within this framework does not rely on a rectilinear grid—a point boldly made by a paved terrace that juts out at an angle from the house. However, it has a purposeful order, which faceted topiary and other features that close views help to achieve.

A swimming pool is notoriously attention-seeking. One solution is reverential display; but the option taken here is to enclose it. The buttressed yew hedges that screen it and a working kitchen garden embrace in their curves a calm area of lawn. The buttresses create niches for a garden seat and a piece of sculpture. The mass of the hedges is lightened by the portals cut in them and the white trunk of a birch (*Betula utilis* var. *jacquemontii*) shows dramatically against the dark green. An avenue of pleached lindens (*Tilia platyphyllos* 'Rubra') makes a formal approach to the pool through the swing doors of the changing-room.

The busiest parts of the garden are approached from the terrace through a topiary garden. This is of irregular shape but an arrangement of boxwood shapes—triple crescent and triple dot patterns drawn from Ottoman fabrics—creates a balanced although not symmetrical layout. A path through an arch in a hornbeam hedge runs through the kitchen garden to a seat under a Portugal laurel. A conference of topiary cats marks the route, their sleek shapes like that of the Ancient Egyptian cat god Bastet.

Swagged Rambler roses on ropes line an avenue through the most floral part of the garden. Beyond the hornbeam hedge, running between the kitchen and cutting gardens, the path passes under arches supporting cordon apples and pears.

1   *Campis* x *tagliabuana* 'Mme Galen'
2   Container-grown faceted topiary shape in yew
3   *Betula utilis* var. *jacquemontii*
4   Curved yew hedge with buttresses
5   Curved yew hedge with buttresses and ball finials
6   Avenue of pleached red-twigged linden (*Tilia platyphyllos* 'Rubra')
7   Boxwood hedge
8   Hedge of holly (*Ilex aquifolium* 'J.C. van Tol')
9   1 of 4 containers planted with dwarf boxwood trimmed as low drums
10 1 of 2 clusters of pots planted with scented-leaved pelargoniums and summer-flowering annuals
11 Holly hedge (see 8)

12 1 of 4 arches supporting cordon-trained pears and apples
13 1 of 4 topiary yew cats
14 Cutting garden
15 Ornamental kitchen garden
16 Angled topiary shape in yew
17 Summer-flowering border
18 Rope swags and arch supporting Rambler roses
19 1 of 2 sets of beds, each set consisting of 3 boxwood-edged beds, and a boxwood column rising from a seasonal planting giving them a crescent shape
20 Hornbeam hedge with two arched openings
21 1 of 4 sets of drum topiary shapes in boxwood, each set consisting of 3 drums
22 Faceted topiary shape in yew

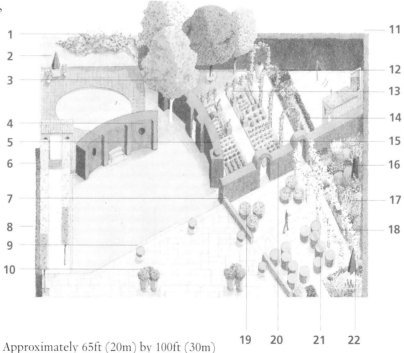

Approximately 65ft (20m) by 100ft (30m)

Climbers as screens and canopies

Climbers are a large group of plants that in the wild rely for the most part on other plants to support them in their race to the light. Many, like the common honeysuckle (*Lonicera periclymenum*), are twiners, the twining action powered by the cells on the outside of the stem growing more quickly than those on the inside. Others, including annual sweet peas (*Lathyrus odoratus*), have parts of their structure specially adapted as tendrils, which lash the climber to its support. The common ivy is the best-known plant of temperate regions that attaches itself to its support by aerial roots (see page 70) but many more examples can be found in tropical forests. Various hook devices help another range of climbers. The vigorous Rambler roses, for example, grow rapidly, their thorns catching in tangled growth and preventing the stems from slipping backward.

The idea of using climbers ornamentally probably developed from training for practical purposes. A pergola was commonly used in the ancient world for training grapevines, and valued as a light and airy structure that cast a delicious shade. The appeal of garden architecture carrying climbers is fully evident in wall paintings from Pompeii dating from the 1st century A.D. The appeal is undiminished today and in modern gardens of small or medium size a built structure billowing with climbers making a screen or canopy is a more controllable three-dimensional feature than a tree or large shrub. A very wide range of climbers is available for tropical and subtropical gardens, and even in temperate regions there is considerable choice that goes well beyond the familiar clematis, roses and wisteria. (See the list of Plants for Special Purposes in the Directory on page 155.)

Supports for climbers

House walls, boundary walls and fences provide scope for growing many climbers. A sunny wall creates a favorable microclimate for tender plants, including wall shrubs. A support system is needed for all but ivy and other self-clinging climbers. Galvanized gauge No. 12 wires, run horizontally and spaced about 20in (50cm) apart, can be attached to vine eyes so that they stand out at least 2in (5cm) from the wall. A vertical system of wires suits twiners even better. Panels of trellis make more conspicuous supports. When these are fixed to a wall there should be a gap of about 2in (5cm) between

panel and wall; they can also be used with a system of posts to make freestanding screens. The various kinds of netting and mesh available are generally less pleasing aesthetically.

The arbor is the most effective support for large-scale overhead training. It is often a major architectural feature in its own right, its powerful tunnel-like axis, fringed with shade-loving plants, linking one part of the garden to another. Particularly in small and medium-size gardens, the arbor often extends from the house, creating a shaded outdoor room. The typical structure consists of evenly spaced paired uprights running on each side of a path and supporting beams running parallel with the path; the beams in turn support a flat open roof composed of crosspieces. There are many variations on this theme. The uprights may be of wood, brick, masonry or metal. To strengthen the roof and to simplify training there may be additional beams running lengthwise and also a system of wires. An arbor-like structure can be composed of a series of linked arches.

Although a much simpler architectural feature, the arch also makes a strong three-dimensional accent that, as well as providing support for plants, is often highly ornamental in itself. Climbers can also be trained on other airy structures, often built of lattice-work, that give shade or serve as eye-catchers; the categories of arbor, bower, gazebo and pavilion melt into one another. Lattice-work pyramids and obelisks too, sometimes used as formal sculptural entities in the garden, can support plants. Pillars with heavy rope looped between them are particularly suited to the pliant growth of Rambler roses. Less permanent but highly ornamental supports can be made from a range of materials—favorites are wigwams of bamboo canes to carry runner beans and sweet peas.

OPPOSITE Even when the bare stems of Climber and Rambler roses are closely trained to their supports, in summer there is such an explosion of growth that arches and arbors lose their definition among the sprays of foliage and flowers. The looseness of this free growth makes an appealing contrast to the solid shapes of hedges, topiary, and architectural details such as gates.

Pruning and training

The success of climbers as screens or canopies depends on effective pruning and training. Many climbers need little pruning and are easily trained within a given space. Flowering is generally improved when growth is checked by training stems at or near the horizontal, arching them over or twisting them around a support so that they do not simply shoot upward. Pruning is of greatest importance with climbers that flower most freely on young wood and with a number of very vigorous climbers such as wisterias that tend to make growth at the expense of flowers.

When removing old stems to encourage new growth, correct timing is vital. Climbers that flower on growth produced in the current season are normally pruned in winter or early spring, before growth starts. Climbers that flower on wood produced the previous year are pruned immediately after flowering. The clematis are in this respect a mixed group. Spring-flowering species and hybrids such as *Clematis alpina* are cut back or, in the case of the vigorous *C. montana*, shorn over after flowering. *C. viticella* and others that flower in summer and fall on growth of the current season are pruned in winter. There are, however, many large-flowered clematis hybrids

OPPOSITE LEFT The lax growth of Rambler roses makes them suitable for training on a wide range of supports. Their flowering season in early to mid-summer is relatively short so it is important that their support system is aesthetically pleasing. In this trellised rose garden, inverted metal arches seem to hang weightlessly, the roses trained on their drooping curves forming elegant swags.

OPPOSITE RIGHT Ornamental gourds are a sensational alternative to sweet peas (*Lathyrus odoratus*) and other annuals grown for their flowers. Annuals with strongly surging upward growth need little pruning and training, but the support system, whether wigwams of bamboo canes, columns of brushwood or, as here, a permanent framework of metal arches, must be securely anchored and sturdy enough to bear the weight of growth and withstand buffeting by wind.

RIGHT The common honeysuckle (*Lonicera periclymenum*) has for centuries been a favorite climber in European gardens, often trained to form bowers and arbors because of the sweetness of its flowers. The more vigorous *L. × italica*, shown here, also fragrant, can be used in the same way.

TRAINING WISTERIA ON AN ARBOR

The wisterias in general cultivation are all vigorous climbers. If left to their own devices they produce numerous long twining stems and are often slow to reach flowering maturity. You can encourage flowering with horizontal training and a pruning regime that develops the short spurs where flower buds are produced. Formative pruning differs slightly for wall-trained and standard wisterias but for mature plants the summer/winter regime is the same for all.

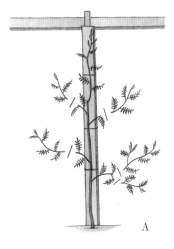

A

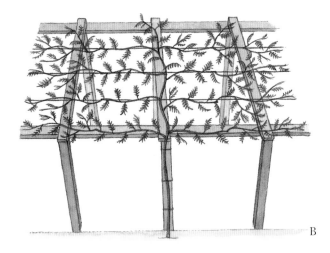

B

MATERIALS REQUIRED

1 young wisteria, such as *Wisteria sinensis*—seed-raised wisterias are very variable and it is best to buy a named cultivar, with a strong main stem

Sturdily built arbor with wires 12–18in (30–45cm) apart running horizontally the length of the arbor between crossbeams

Adjustable ties

Hand pruners; loppers

FORMATIVE PRUNING

1 Plant between mid-fall and early spring at the base of an upright, ideally where there is scope for training out a framework of branches left and right at the top of the arbor. Do not twist the stem around the support but tie it in securely, using several ties if necessary.

2 Shorten the leader by about one-third, cutting back to a strong bud, and remove side shoots.

3 In the summer, train up the leader, securing it to its support, and shorten side shoots by about two-thirds. (A)

4 In winter, shorten the main stem, cutting at a strong bud 6–12in (15–30cm) above the height of the arbor, and remove all side shoots below the height of the arbor.

5 In the following summer, continue training the leader, taking it over the top edge of the arbor and tying it and any well-placed side shoots suitable as arms for the framework to wires.

6 In the following winter, cut back the leader to within about 18in (45cm) of the height of the top edge of the arbor and shorten by about one-third the side shoots that have been tied in.

7 In the subsequent summers and winters continue developing a framework of branches, cutting out growth that is superfluous and combining this with a regime of pruning to encourage flowering spurs (see below). (B)

C

PRUNING THE MATURE PLANT

A regime of summer and winter pruning begins as soon as the formation of the framework has started.

1 Two to three weeks after mid-summer, cut back growth not wanted as framework branches at about 6in (15cm), leaving four to six of the composite leaves. (C)

2 In winter, remove all secondary growth from the main stem and the framework branches and shorten the growth that was cut back in summer to about 4in (10cm), leaving two to three buds. (D)

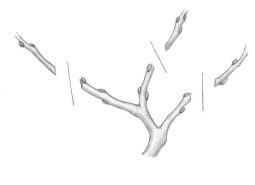

D

SUMMER PRUNING

WINTER PRUNING

Wisterias have no difficulty climbing into tall trees but the effect of the flowers, clustered in drooping racemes, is partly lost. The flowers are seen to better effect when wisterias are trained horizontally on arbors and at a reasonable height, when it is possible to prune annually in summer and winter to encourage the development of flowering spurs.

such as 'The President' that flower first on old wood and then later in the same season on new wood. The most satisfactory compromise with these is to cut back only a proportion of the growth in winter.

The regular removal of a proportion of the old stems of Climber and Rambler roses helps to keep them free-flowering. The complex parentage of many roses is such that only general pruning guidelines can be given here. Most of the Ramblers, such as 'Rambling Rector,' produce long flexible stems that can be trained along the top of an arbor or tied to rope loops suspended from pillars. A high proportion of the old stems can be cut out after flowering and new shoots tied in. The repeat-flowering Ramblers and Climbers are pruned between fall and late winter, the laterals that have carried flowers being cut back. The short-growing Climbers, sometimes called "pillar" roses, tend to be stiff and bare at the base. If young stems are flexible enough they should be trained spirally around the support.

The flowers and fruits of many very vigorous climbers are produced on young laterals or from spurs. With these climbers the best method of training is to establish a permanent framework of branches and then to prune annually, removing laterals that have flowered or fruited. You can train the arms of a wisteria framework against a wall or screen as well as horizontally on the roof of an arbor (see page 114). Prune in summer, after flowering, and then again in winter to check growth and promote the development of spurs. Grapevines bear their fruit on young laterals, and techniques for pruning aim at cutting out old laterals and encouraging the development of replacements to bear the next crop. The rod and spur system, for instance, leaves only the permanent framework of the main stem, that is the rod, or several rods, and the stub-like spurs when the laterals are cut back annually in the fall. This system works well on an arbor or screen even when grapes are being grown principally for their ornamental value and can be applied less rigorously to other species of *Vitis*.

Fruit trees as screens and canopies

Spring blossom and the ripening crop that follows make many fruit trees very ornamental. Pruning and training, which play an important part in maintaining good yields, can be used to control growth severely, either to save space or so that the plant benefits from a particularly favorable position against a warm wall. Training of branches at or toward the horizontal checks growth but also encourages the production of flower buds. The restricted forms, particularly tiers and fans in a single plane, that result from such shaping are decorative architectural shapes that you can use in the garden to mark boundaries, as screens and as focal points. They are often kept to the kitchen garden but, as with many other useful plants, you can attractively combine them with ornamentals in the flower garden.

Fruit trees require good growing conditions and in most cases fruit will ripen satisfactorily only when there is adequate exposure to sun. Some fruit trees are self-fertile but most need a suitable pollinator close by in order to produce good crops. In the case of some fruit trees, particularly apples, the vigor of a particular plant is to some extent controlled by the rootstock on which the cultivar is grafted or budded. To train a restricted form of an apple tree, for example, you should use a cultivar on a dwarfing or semi-dwarfing rootstock.

Ornamental shrubs can also be trained as tiers or fans. As with fruit trees a framework of branches is developed over several years and excessive growth on the mature shape is checked by summer pruning. Several popular shrubs include firethorns (*Pyracantha*), which make handsome espaliers, the arms loaded with orange, red or yellow fruit for many weeks in fall and winter; and Japanese quinces, which respond well to training as fans grown against walls or trellis (as in the garden illustrated on page 69).

LEFT The neat order of a well-run kitchen garden is in itself ornamental. In this garden, sheltered by hedges and divided into beds by brick paths, wigwams are being prepared for climbing beans as fruit trees come into flower. Espaliered apples border paths while cordon pears, trained over an arch, form a bower.

OPPOSITE Trained and shaped plants underscore the geometric layout of this garden. Low boxwood hedges, with topiary accents of domes and cones, line the paths. Standard roses are just coming into leaf. The highlight in spring is the blossom of apple trees, espaliered in one or four tiers.

TRAINING A THREE-TIERED APPLE ESPALIER

These instructions are for training an espalier in the open garden supported by a system of posts and wires.
In the early stages the stems are tied to bamboo canes fixed to the wires, not to the wires themselves.

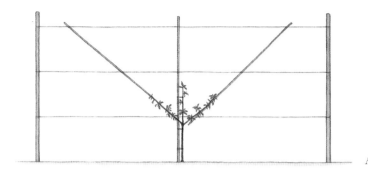

A

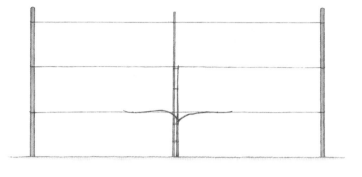

B

MATERIALS REQUIRED

Unfeathered maiden apple tree (one that has not yet developed a branching system) on a dwarfing or semi-dwarfing rootstock

A support system, 10–13ft (3–4m) long, on well-prepared ground consisting of two endposts to which are fixed three horizontal wires, the bottom one 18in (45cm) above ground level and the two above it equally spaced 16–18in (40–45cm) apart

3 bamboo canes about 5ft (1.5m) long

Tarred string; ties

Hand pruners; pruning knife

1 Between late fall and late winter, plant the young tree.
2 After planting, cut back the stem just above a bud at approximately the height of the lowest wire, ensuring that there are another two buds to the left and right below it to form the bottom arms of the espalier.

3 During the following summer, train the shoot from the top bud vertically, tying it to a cane inserted vertically into the ground beside the plant and fixed to the wires.
4 At the same time, train the shoots from the two lower buds to left and right, tying each to canes tied to the wires at an angle of 45°. (A)

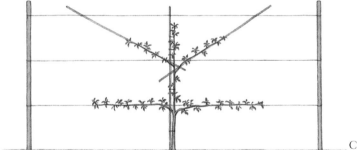

C

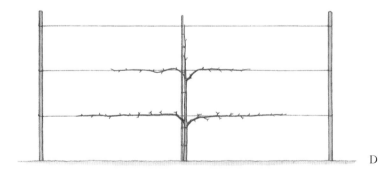

D

5 In the fall of the same year, carefully lower the branches (formed from these shoots) so that they extend horizontally and tie them to the lowest wire, removing the canes.
6 At the same time, shorten the central leader, cutting it just above the middle wire, ensuring there are three good buds—two for the arms and the topmost to

extend the main trunk (ideally on the opposite side to the stem cut the previous year). (B)
7 In the following summer, train the arms of the second tier, as in step 4. Continue training the leader vertically, as in step 3. (C)
8 At the same time, begin summer pruning by cutting back shoots on the arms of the bottom tier to three or four leaves.

9 In the following fall, lower the arms of the second tier and tie onto the wire, removing the canes. Cut back the main stem above a bud near the top wire, ensuring that there are two buds below it. (D)
10 In the following summer, train out two arms as in step 4 to form the top tier, using canes extending above the main

framework. Continue summer-pruning laterals on the horizontal arms and remove any vigorous upright shoots.
11 In the fall, lower the topmost arms to the horizontal and tie onto the upper wire. Cut back the lower arms if they are the required length. Remove the vertical cane. The pruning of the spur system is described on page 119.

The combination of fruit trees and vegetables with ornamentals is an attractive idea for a small garden. Apples and pears are the most versatile fruit trees for growing in a confined space as they respond well to training in restricted forms. The initial pruning and training develops the desired shape, which in the case of this apple tree, growing on a dwarfing or semi-dwarfing rootstock, is a three-tiered espalier. Like other restricted forms, the established espalier is pruned in summer, to control vegetative growth and to encourage the development of the spur systems that carry the fruit.

Espaliers and cordons

The espalier and cordon are restricted forms well suited to the training of apples and pears, which in broad terms respond to the same methods of pruning. The espalier consists of a main stem supporting one or several tiers—rarely more than five—of paired branches trained out horizontally to left and right. Whether grown against a wall or fence or in the open garden, it has a permanent system of posts and wires to support the tiers. A single-tier espalier makes an attractive edging 12–18in (30–45cm) high, while a multi-tier espalier can be treated as a formal screen to border a path and to make divisions within a garden (as in the productive garden illustrated on page 123).

The formative pruning of an espalier is described and illustrated opposite. The mature espalier needs to be pruned in summer to check its growth and to encourage the development of the spurs, which produce flower buds, beginning in the first summer that arms are growing out horizontally, but the fruit should not be allowed to develop until the tree has been established for three years. Leave pruning until after mid-summer, and then cut long laterals back to three leaves above the basal cluster. You can leave short laterals, under about 8in (20cm) in length, unpruned as they are likely to form flower buds. Cut back any sub-laterals growing from the spur system to one leaf. When spur systems become congested they should be thinned in winter. Little other winter pruning is necessary except to remove any growth made after the summer pruning.

The cordon, in its simplest form, consists of a single stem furnished over most of its length with fruiting spurs. It is very often grown at an angle of about 45°; several oblique cordons may be spaced 30–36in (75–90cm) apart to form a row permanently supported on a system of posts and wires. This method of training can form a highly productive fruit screen, with a number of trees being grown in a small space and cropping well, partly because the oblique training checks vigor and encourages the production of fruit buds. Cordons are sometimes trained vertically and occasionally with two or more parallel arms to make virtuosic displays of a kind much favored in 19th-century gardens. The cordon is summer-pruned in the same way as an espalier, the aim of pruning being to restrict growth and encourage the development of spurs.

Fans

Apples and pears are occasionally grown as fans, against a wall or on a support system in the open garden. However, the method is mainly used for stone fruits, such as peaches and apricots, and figs. In temperate gardens with relatively cool, short summers the fruits of these trees may not ripen satisfactorily unless the position is favorably sunny and the fruit ripening process is boosted by the reflected heat of a warm wall. Another advantage of trained fruit plants is that fans are more easily netted to prevent bird damage than fruit bushes.

The formative pruning of fans, usually on a system of wire supports, is much the same for all fruits. The structure of the fan is based on two arms at a height of about 12in (30cm), trained out on each side of the main stem at an angle of 45°. The arms are stimulated into growth by cutting back the main stem of the newly planted young tree above two buds, one facing to the left and the other to the right. Over several years well-placed shoots that develop from the arms are trained to form the ribs of the fan. Growth that projects forward or back and cannot be trained into the plane of the fan is cut out. Once established, different trees have special pruning requirements to maintain free-flowering and fruitful fans. Acid cherries, nectarines and peaches are pruned on renewal systems: once a lateral has fruited, cut it out and train in a replacement. Prune apricots, sweet and duke cherries and plums to encourage the development of fruiting spurs: pinch back shoots in summer to six or seven leaves and shorten to three buds in winter. Figs are capable of producing two or three crops a year but in cool temperate regions the aim of pruning is to ensure one good crop. Pinch back growth in the first half of summer to encourage the development of shoots that will bear fruit and cut back wood after the figs have been harvested to prevent growth from becoming too crowded.

Fruit tunnels and arches

Fruit arches and tunnels exploit the ornamental value of fruit trees grown in restricted forms. Apples and pears are the most versatile fruit trees, and pears are easier to train on a curve than apples. The simplest approach is to provide a permanent structure of sturdy

arched metal supports over which a pair of cordons can be trained, one cordon from each side. A sequence of arches planted in this way can make a highly decorative feature in the kitchen garden (as in the garden illustrated on page 109). An extended arched frame over a path could also be planted with espaliers on either side, with the stems trained up main supports and the arms along struts running lengthwise so that instead of forming a vertical plane the espaliers follow the curve of the framework. As with conventional espaliers and cordons, summer pruning is essential. It controls vegetative growth and develops the spurs that bear flowers and subsequently fruit.

OPPOSITE In temperate gardens, fruit trees suitable for training as fans, among them apricots and peaches, are usually grown against a warm wall, where the favorable microclimate helps the fruit to ripen in cool summers. Where summers are so short and cool that even apples and pears grown in the open garden do not readily ripen, the wall training of restricted forms, including fans, is the best way of ensuring that crops mature. Where the climate is milder, fans of apples or pears, like espaliers of these fruits, make attractive screens in the open garden.

RIGHT This kitchen garden, sheltered by a yew hedge, is divided into compartments by brick paths lined with boxwood and lavender hedging. Rustic arches made from hazel poles have been erected as supports for climbing beans. Although relatively temporary, supports such as these arches and wigwams of bamboo canes can be highly decorative features in a garden that is productive and ornamental.

Decorative order in a productive garden

In the kitchen garden illustrated here, enclosed for protection, fruits, vegetables and herbs are arranged in an orderly way that makes economical use of space, simplifies cultivation and ensures a seasonal succession of crops, and creates an attractive design.

The productive garden measures approximately 70ft (21m) by 46ft (14m) and is laid out as a compartment within a larger garden. Its most distinctive feature is a central boxwood-edged square set at an angle within the rectangular plot and there are focal points that keep the garden self-contained. This formula lends itself to many treatments. It could be used where the rectangle is the complete garden, and with a radically different balance of ornamental and useful plants. For example, the central square of the garden might be planted exclusively with ornamentals and the area outside it used for growing espaliered fruit trees, soft fruits, vegetables and herbs.

The main access to the garden is from the left, and a path leads through to a garden seat backed by a curved yew hedge. The central square consists of four raised beds outlined with brick paving. There is a checkerboard pattern of cultivation in each bed and their formality is underlined by espaliered apple trees, oriented to get plenty of sun. Those along the main axis have a single tier and those parallel to the axis, at the other ends of the beds, have three.

The area outside the boxwood-bordered square includes a graveled open space. A wall in the foreground (not shown in the illustration) would provide an ideal support for a fan-trained acid cherry, which does not require a position in full sun to ripen its fruit. A row of topiary cones and water tanks runs parallel to the main axis, while a mature crab apple standing beside a small garden shed makes a focal point terminating the garden's secondary axis. This leads through the central square, past a formal planting of standard gooseberries, to a metal arch supporting cordon pears. Larger fruit and vegetable crops, a collection of culinary herbs and flowers for cutting have all been accommodated outside the square.

LEFT A "step-over" apple espalier—a low single tier—and a standard gooseberry are ornamental and productive features in a thickly planted garden.

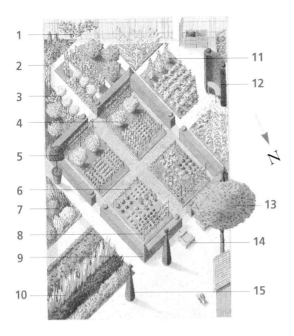

1 Loganberry
2 Arch supporting cordon-trained pears
3 1 of 6 standard gooseberries underplanted
   with alpine strawberries in area devoted
   to soft fruit
4 1 of 4 red currant bushes
5 Pot-grown standard bay laurel
6 1 of 4 single-tier espaliered apples
7 Herb garden
8 1 of 4 three-tier espaliered apples
9 Boxwood hedge with openings on all four
   sides, ball finials at the openings and pyramid
   finials at the corners, surrounding the
   central part of the kitchen garden, which
   is closely planted with small vegetables
   and salad crops
10 Cutting garden
11 1 of 3 wigwams supporting runner beans
   in an area devoted to large-scale vegetables
12 Curved yew hedge with ball finials
13 Crab apple
14 1 of 2 water tanks with brick surrounds
15 1 of 3 boxwood cones

Approximately 70ft (21m) by 46ft (14m)

Long-lived hedges

Like well-maintained topiary shapes, hedges of classic plants such as boxwood and yew can be very long-lived. Pests and diseases (see page 16 and entries in the Directory, page 148) may occasionally present problems but the greatest threat to a hedge is neglect. A new owner taking over an established garden often faces problems with hedges resulting from poor formative pruning and past failure to clip regularly. Moreover, even well-maintained hedges have a way of growing so that the small increments of growth made each year eventually produce hedges that are very much wider than their original shape.

Common problems

Correct timing of pruning (see entries in the Directory, page 148) will minimize some of the common problems of hedges. Untypically early or late frosts and cold winds may cause the foliage to scorch but you can remove superficial damage by clipping. Where a plant has failed, perhaps because of drought, it is relatively easy to insert a replacement in a new hedge. It is useful to have a few spares of the selected clone planted in a piece of spare ground at the same time as the hedge in case of failures. When planting a replacement, even at an early stage, dig out and replace old soil. It is a much more difficult matter to replace a plant that has failed in an established hedge. In such cases it is important to discover the cause of the failure; one plant failing often heralds an overall decline in the health of a hedge. The underlying cause might be poor drainage, compaction of the soil or a disease such as honey fungus. If this is so, with an established hedge the best course is often to remove the dead or dying plant and to train neighboring plants to fill the gap, tying replacement shoots into position with tarred string. The same method can be used to fill holes in hedges. Patchy growth often indicates that a hedge is starved of nutrients—a problem that can be put right by regular applications of a slow-release fertilizer in spring.

Irregularities in growth over the length of a hedge are frequently caused by shading or damage caused by accumulations of snow in winter. Clear heavy falls of snow before they have a chance to cause damage, and where possible remove overhead branches and growths leaning into a hedge. Gappiness at the base of a hedge may be caused by shading from the hedge itself, particularly on hedges clipped without a batter, but the problem is often the result of a failure to cut back young plants, particularly of boxwood, at an early stage in the development of a hedge. There are no ready solutions when the hedge is mature, although a reasonably successful patching job can sometimes be done by planting fillers along the base.

Neglected and overgrown hedges

If you have newly taken over a garden with neglected and overgrown hedges, you will have to take hard decisions. It is often possible to rescue a hedge, especially a slow-growing one, that has suffered a few years of neglect. Corrective trimming, clearing weeds from the hedge bottom, and the application of a slow-release fertilizer and if possible a mulch are often enough to restore a hedge to a healthy and vigorous condition. Old and neglected hedges of the fast-growing privet are often taken out and replaced but in fact can sometimes be rescued by hard pruning.

Occasionally a very old hedge, although regularly clipped, has lost its original shape and acquired a mysterious personality all its own. It might be possible to restore such a hedge to its original formality, although the older the hedge the greater the risks involved in restoration that calls for heavy pruning. A restored hedge would certainly be easier to clip, but it is probably better to retain a hedge of unique character, provided it is healthy and vigorous, even though trimming it is time-consuming. Sometimes a hedge has fallen into such a state of dereliction that the only sensible course is to take it out. The ground needs to be well

OPPOSITE It is not always clear what has caused the swelling and dipping surfaces of old yew hedges, as in these monumental examples on the terraces at Powis Castle in Wales, but it is likely that past damage to shoots is a factor—perhaps by squirrels and even mice, who, despite the toxicity of yew, will sometimes gnaw the bark around a stem, causing it to die back. Hedges with such an irregular shape are certainly time-consuming and difficult to trim, but they have their own beauty and to attempt their renovation would require a stern preference for order.

The superb maintenance of these beech hedges and arches will help ensure
their long life. A major part of the regime is regular trimming and the removal
of clippings, which can harbor diseases. The annual application of a slow-release
fertilizer will promote healthy growth. Eventually hedges thicken, encroaching
on beds and becoming increasingly time-consuming to clip. Overgrown beech
hedges usually respond well to renovation staged over several years.

RENOVATING AN OVERGROWN YEW HEDGE

The yew hedge illustrated (A) has grown to a height of 11½ft (3.5m) and the width has extended to nearly 8ft (2.5m). The aim is to reduce the height to 8ft (2.5m) and the width of the base to 4ft (1.2m), the sides being cut with a batter so that the top is 24in (60cm) wide. Although old yew hedges are remarkably resilient, drastic pruning to renovate should be staged over several years. The hedge should be mulched and fertilized the year before renovation, and all ivy removed. A delay of two years is suggested before the second side of the hedge is cut back, but it may be necessary to wait another year if growth is slow to develop on the side that has been cut.

MATERIALS REQUIRED
Trestles and planks; ladder
Pruning saw; loppers; shears; hand pruners

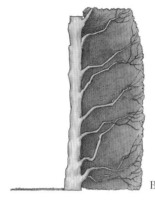

A B C D

1 A year before cutting back, apply a slow-release general fertilizer and an organic mulch. Remove any ivy.
2 In early spring, trim one side of the hedge lightly. Cut back the top to the required height and cut all growth on the untrimmed side right back to the main stem. (B)
3 In mid- to late spring of the following year, trim the top and lightly clip the side that has yet to be cut back severely.
4 Apply a slow-release general fertilizer and replenish the mulch.
5 In mid- to late spring of the following year, trim the top and then cut back to the trunk on the side that has not yet been severely pruned. (C)

6 Apply a slow-release fertilizer and an organic mulch.
7 In the summer of the following year, begin trimming the sides to the required dimensions to encourage growth to thicken up and to re-establish a batter. (D)

---

cultivated and generous quantities of organic manure should be added before another hedge is planted on the same site. The new hedging plant should be different from the one taken out. This minimizes the risk of failure that sometimes occurs as a result of replanting in ground that has previously had the same plant growing in it. To avoid a gap, where there is room, it is worth delaying the removal of an old hedge and planting a replacement hedge parallel to it, 5ft (1.5m) from the original, and removing the old hedge only when the new one is established.

There is a good chance of rescuing overgrown hedges of boxwood and yew if they have become very overgrown, although success cannot be guaranteed, especially where winters are harsh.

The drastic treatment described above to renovate yew does not work with all hedging plants, but others that respond with varying degrees of success include beech and hornbeam (see also entries in the Directory, page 148). The best chance of renovating boxwood is to trim the plant back to a framework of branches but not right back to the main stem. The major variation in the renovation of hedging plants is in the timing: cut back deciduous hedges hard in late winter, evergreens in early spring. Staging the drastic pruning over several years and generous feeding and mulching, and watering in spells of dry weather, give the best chance of success, particularly if weeds are cleared and feeding and mulching begin the year before plants are cut back.

PATTERNED PLANTING

Knots, embroidered parterres and beds

Knot gardens with geometric patterns

Embroidered and figurative designs

An Art Deco garden

Simple beds and compartments

Mazes

The knot garden at Helmingham Hall in Suffolk is in keeping
with the Tudor mansion, the flowers and herbs inside the
low boxwood hedges being plants grown in English gardens
in the late 16th and early 17th centuries.

Knots, embroidered parterres and beds

Pattern and symmetry produced by the repetition of line or decorative motif are found in some of the earliest examples of human crafts. They have also been conspicuous features of garden layouts from the earliest times, employed for utilitarian as well as artistic reasons. The basis of most symmetrical and patterned layouts is the division of gardens into compartments. The kitchen garden, laid out with little beds, stands out as one of the most appealing models. In more elaborate schemes, both ornamental and useful, the beds are defined by brick or masonry surrounds or by low hedging. No plant has been more widely used for edging beds than the common boxwood, and especially the dwarf cultivar *Buxus sempervirens* 'Suffruticosa,' which seems to have originated in Holland toward the end of the 16th century. A patterned layout characteristic of many periods consists of regular, simple beds of ornamental or useful plants enclosed by low hedges.

Other kinds of patterning are associated with specific historical developments in gardening. Knot gardens are particularly associated with Elizabethan and Jacobean England. These designs followed the intricate patterns of embroidery, which also featured in bookbinding and plasterwork; the planting and shaping of the knot suggested the "over and under" of worked thread. Embroidered patterns or parterres, *parterres de broderie*, are a kind of patterned planting typical of 17th-century French gardening in the grand manner; they combine severity and elegance, with clipped boxwood—set against plain earth or a colored ground—unfurling in a richly scrolled design. The maze, too, is particularly associated with 17th-century gardens. These forms of patterning in gardens all have in common the fact that they depend in some way on the shaping of plants.

LEFT A calligraphic flourish in dwarf boxwood and mysterious punctuation in boxwood cones and balls are set against gravel.

OPPOSITE Compartments of boxwood enclose spring-flowering tulips growing through forget-me-nots. An adaptation of 19th-century bedding in which beds laid out in a pattern are filled with seasonal flowers works well in different scales.

Knot gardens with geometric patterns

A knot garden can be created without specialist skills and fits happily into a small plot. Many existing knot gardens, with under-and-over designs, are distinctive and historically authentic, using versions of designs published by writers such as Thomas Hill (*The Gardener's Labyrinth*, 1577) and William Lawson (*The Countrie Housewife's Garden*, 1617). Such designs are obviously appropriate with buildings of the period, but the self-contained and mesmeric character of knots makes them easy to place in many settings, whatever the architecture. Rather than extend the scale of a knot, it is better to repeat the pattern.

Some patterns that seem to have held a particular fascination for gardeners in the late 16th and early 17th centuries are dauntingly intricate, but the modern gardener may use any interweaving design. The simpler Celtic designs, for instance, such as the continuous interweaving of a King Solomon's knot, provide a rich source of ideas and could form the basis of plaited designs for square and rectangular beds. Other ideas that could be developed are sinuous overlapping ogee networks of the kind used so spectacularly in Ottoman fabrics, Islamic geometric and Chinese lattice patterns; or an intriguing Japanese paper knot, difficult to untie and so symbolic of love and marriage. Some variations on basketweave are also worth translating into patterns of plants.

Although boxwood is widely used in knot gardens today, it seems that it did not feature prominently until the early 17th century. In old knot gardens hyssop, rue (*Ruta graveolens*), lavender, cotton lavender, rosemary and thyme (*Thymus vulgaris*), and other shrubby herbs were used to form the interweaving lines. Making a knot with aromatic herbs remains an attractive option; but other shrubs that are naturally compact, such as *Berberis thunbergii* 'Globe,' or plants that take regular trimming, among them *Lonicera nitida*, can be used for the pattern. A range of plants to include in knot gardens is listed in the Directory (see Plants for Special Purposes, page 154). Different-colored earths and a curious range of other materials, including even bones and coal, were frequently used as colored grounds to show off the pattern. The alternative was to plant between the interweaving lines. Despite the great flood of plant introductions to Western gardens since the 17th century, many of the flowers known then have remained firm favorites. It is still possible to plant a garden with cultivars of pinks and tulips, to mention just two plants that bear a strong resemblance to the kinds treasured in old gardens. If flowers are not to be grown in the gaps, the easiest material for the modern gardener to use as background to the pattern is a mulch of gravel. Choose an appropriate color and lay it over plastic sheeting or polythene to prevent weeds from coming through.

The success of a knot garden, as for all patterns using shaped plants, depends very much on the thoroughness of the preparatory work. Start with a design, carefully drawn to scale on graph paper, that will fit the space available. For plants to make even growth the site needs to be in an open position on well-drained ground. An ideal setting for a knot garden is a raised bed, neatly finished with boards to a height of about 4in (10cm). Dig the ground thoroughly and incorporate organic material such as well-rotted garden compost in advance of planting. This preparation is best done in the early fall; allow the bed to settle and then level it ready for planting between fall and early spring.

A relatively simple design—such as that for a knot illustrated on page 134—can be transferred from paper to ground by marking straight lengths for planting with garden line, and curves using garden line like a compass, one end fixed, the other, with a stake or cane attached at the appropriate distance, scratching a shallow furrow as the line is swung in an arc. Transferring a more complex design from paper to ground is still best done as it was in Tudor and Jacobean gardens. In this method lines spaced at regular intervals, say 20in (50cm) apart, running lengthwise and crosswise over the bed, make a grid that corresponds to the lines of the graph paper on which the design is drawn. You can mark out the lines of the design on the bed square by square, either with dry sand dribbled from a bottle or with a water-based spray paint.

OPPOSITE An under-and-over knot of boxwood, planted in a square of gravel and shown off by low light, forms the centerpiece of this garden compartment, divided into quarters by brick paths. The layout's success depends on the contrast between the tight knot pattern and the loose but vigorous and rich planting of the main beds.

LAYING OUT A KNOT GARDEN WITH AN UNDER-AND-OVER DESIGN

The under-and-over design of this simple knot garden is in the style of patterns popular in gardens in 16th- and early 17th-century England, and its plants are similar to those that were then used. The outer square of dwarf boxwood (Buxus sempervirens 'Suffruticosa') contains an inner square of pink hyssop (Hyssopus officinalis f. roseus) and semicircular arcs of a dwarf lavender (Lavandula angustifolia 'Hidcote'). At the center is a drum of common boxwood (Buxus sempervirens). The pattern is strong enough to need no other planting but spring and summer flowers could fill the gaps. It is assumed that the site for this knot has been marked out and prepared as a raised bed 11½ft (3.6m) square, well dug, manured and leveled, in readiness for planting between fall and early spring.

MATERIALS REQUIRED

Scale drawing of the proposed knot garden (as shown in the illustration)

Plants: minimum 7 dozen dwarf boxwood, 3 dozen hyssop, 6 dozen lavender and 1 common boxwood (species as above)

116ft (35m) of garden line

18 stakes or sturdy bamboo canes about 18in (45cm) high

Gravel

Spade; trowel

1 To mark the inner edges of the boxwood border, set stakes on the outer edges at 12in (30cm) from each corner in both directions (a), and run garden line between opposite pairs of stakes.
2 Measure and then mark with a stake the midpoint of the inner edge of the boxwood border on each of the four sides (b).
3 Measure 6in (15cm) in from each midpoint along lines temporarily stretched in a cross between opposite midpoints, and mark with stakes (c).
4 Mark the center of the knot with a stake (d) and then take away the lines stretched between the midpoints.
5 To mark the line for planting the hyssop that will make the inner square, run a line (e) between the four stakes set in from the midpoints.

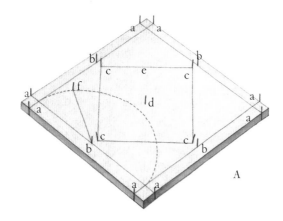

6 To mark the planting line of the first lavender semicircular arc (f) (one of the four that cross over and under the hyssop square), attach one end of a line to the midpoint stake and the other to a stake or cane (f), the line being 4½ft (1.4m). Moving the taut line around the central point, scratch a semicircular line in the earth. (A) Following the same procedure, mark out the planting lines for the other three lavender arcs.
7 Remove the stake marking the center of the knot and plant the specimen of common boxwood.
8 Plant the lavender in the first semicircular arc, beginning on the left. Space the plants regularly, about 10in (25cm) apart but, where the hyssop and lavender planting lines meet in the second half of the arc, plant at 10in (25cm) from each side of the hyssop planting line (g). When the plants develop it will seem that at this point the line of lavender goes under the hyssop. (B)
9 Plant lavender in the other three arcs in the same way.

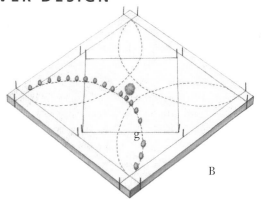

10 Using a cane or stake, scratch a mark along the lines in position for the planting line for the inner square and then remove the lines before planting the hyssop, starting at the corners. Space the plants regularly about 10in (25cm) apart but, where the hyssop is designed to go "under" the lavender, plant at 10in (25cm) from each side of the lavender planting line.
11 Mark a line at the center of the outer square and plant with boxwood, starting at the corners and spacing the plants regularly at about 6in (15cm).
12 Remove all lines and stakes, apply a mulch about 2–3in (5–8cm) deep of clean gravel around the plants and over the whole bed, and then water thoroughly. (C)

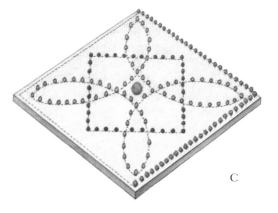

MAINTAINING THE KNOT

1 The hyssop and lavender can be allowed to grow to a height of 16in (40cm), old growth being trimmed back annually in early spring.
2 Trim the boxwood annually in the second half of the summer to a height of approximately 12in (30cm).
3 Trim the boxwood drum in the center annually in the second half of the summer to a height of 24in (60cm) and a diameter of 20in (50cm).

ABOVE In this knot garden the beds are simple boxwood squares with diagonals, a ball-topped standard at each center and cones in boxwood marking the corners. A variegated cultivar of *Euonymus fortunei* has been trained as low standards.

RIGHT One shape in the inner bed of this knot is superimposed on the other, forming four compartments filled with tulips. The inner shape is planted with crown imperials (*Fritillaria imperialis*).

Embroidered and figurative designs

In classic French gardens of the 17th century the full splendor of embroidered parterres was appreciated from the upper floors of a château. However, unlike knot gardens, with their static and self-contained geometry, the scroll patterns of embroidered parterres—usually based on flower and leaf motifs and executed in dwarf boxwood on a ground providing a contrast of color—have an energy that carries the eye outward; in the grandest schemes such patterns are conceived as a prelude to a landscape of heroic perspectives. The design was usually based on two rectangular compartments or two pairs on each side of a central axis, the asymmetrical scroll pattern on one side mirrored in the other. In the 17th century it would usually have been given additional weight and complexity by the inclusion of broad lines, *grands traits*, consisting of bands of grass running through the boxwood scrolls. The whole design was usually surrounded by a border edged with dwarf boxwood. This *plate-bande*, as it was known, which might consist of flowerbeds or mown grass, was commonly punctuated with topiary, statuary or containers for plants.

For those who have the opportunity to lay out an embroidered design in the grand manner—the difficulties are essentially those of scale and expense—the design must first be drawn to scale. It is then transferred to prepared ground, well drained and in an open position, by the traditional method (see page 132), a grid of lines across the ground corresponding to the lines of the graph. It is best to plant the outline of the design first and then fill it in. Dwarf boxwood makes a dense pattern when the plants are spaced about 6in (15cm) apart. As with knot gardens, you can use gravel or chippings of various colors for the ground, with an underlay of plastic sheeting to prevent weeds from getting through. The established pattern can usually be maintained with a single trim a year, in the second half of summer; be sure to sweep the clipped growth off the plants. Laying sheets of burlap or similar material around the pattern before trimming simplifies the job of gathering up the clippings.

For the grandiose schemes of the 17th century to be relevant to small or medium-size gardens, they have to be simplified or plundered for details. Even the most basic version is best seen from a vantage point; small details with flowing lines can make pleasing decorations in many corners of a garden but are always best where they can be seen from an elevated position, such as the upper floors of a house. An ideal arrangement is compartments laid out on each side of an approach to a main door. The design might consist of little more than a pair of simple arabesques that are mirror images of each other. The first impulse is usually to establish symmetry, for instance setting matching flourishes on each side of a path at the foot of a flight of steps or planting an ornament composed of paired S-shaped scrolls beneath a window. However, balanced but asymmetrical flourishes are very appealing, especially when used on a small scale. In most gardens, it will not be possible to relate

LEFT The fragrance of the gilliflower or stock (*Matthiola incana*) has made it a favorite flower in patterned plantings since the 16th century.

OPPOSITE The interlocking S-shapes of a pattern in dwarf boxwood are well defined but the plants are as yet mere tufts rising through a gravel bed.

The coat of arms and lettering in the gardens at Pitmedden in Aberdeenshire, Scotland, are crisply detailed in boxwood. No plans survive of the garden created here in the second half of the 17th century; the recreation is based on the record of other gardens of the period, particularly that at the Palace of Holyroodhouse in Edinburgh.

the design to a perspective extending beyond the garden, but the liveliness of a scroll pattern is greatly enhanced if you plan it as part of a vista, terminated by an eye-catcher such as a statue or handsome topiary specimen.

The French formal garden remains the major source of ideas for scrolled designs, even for small gardens. Inspiration might also be found in vigorous Chinese dragon and cloud motifs and in the sinuous decoration of Art Nouveau. Ironwork gates in Art Nouveau style give a good idea of how to design an impressive pattern with two compartments mirroring each other. Perhaps more relevant for the smaller garden are the countless tailpieces that are used pleasingly on the printed page; these have potential as decorative motifs planted in boxwood.

Similar to embroidered parterres are lettered and figurative designs. This broad category of figures laid out in trimmed plants, usually dwarf boxwood, includes family coats of arms, mottoes, the reign dates of monarchs and allusions to historical events. Civic bedding schemes with such designs, fastidiously laid out in compact foliage and flowering plants, belong to much the same tradition. In themselves these layouts, often more curious than

beautiful, may not be symmetrical but they are usually patterned. If there is wording and figures, these are commonly run as a border within low hedges. Lions rampant and other figurative elements that frequently occur in the design of coats of arms are themselves worth using as the central component of knot gardens. Furthermore, they suggest many other possibilities for figurative designs that are particularly well suited to small-scale layouts. Folk art, including stencil designs, provides some of the best ideas for clean, simple, bold shapes that will read well when translated into living material.

Once the design has been transferred from paper to the ground, it can be expressed in outline, like a drawing, or filled in, making a raised but essentially two-dimensional figure. Dwarf boxwood set against a contrasting surface such as a light-colored gravel is the ideal material for both kinds of design. The key to success with these figures is simple stylization. A linear design must be spare and uncluttered; a filled-in design has to have the clarity of a cut-out. As with embroidered parterres, when planting a filled-in design it is best to begin with the outline and then complete it with plants spaced at regular intervals, about 6in (15cm) apart.

SIMPLE PATTERNS FOR SMALL GARDENS

Although the patterned designs that are so pleasing in small gardens and lend themselves to many variations rely heavily on shaped plants, particularly low hedges, topiary and short standards, other components have a part to play, especially all kinds of paving.

1

2

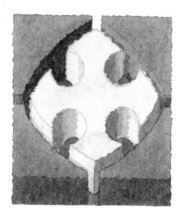

3

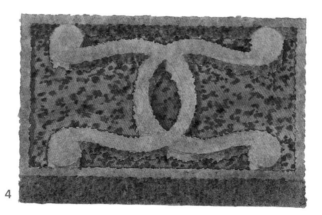

4

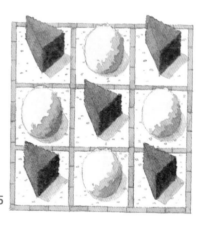

5

1 *Interlocking circles*
The arresting simplicity of a design based on interlocking circles enclosing square terminals shows well in dwarf boxwood set against a plain ground. In this version the total length of the two circles is approximately 10ft (3m) but this is a highly adaptable design. As a garden scheme, it could be executed on a much grander scale, circles and squares in pleached lindens enclosing a grassed interior.

2 *Checked band with standards*
The permanent planting of this checked band consists of dwarf boxwood. The alternating 30in (75cm) squares with a circular central hole, are set in a surround of granite paving blocks, which contain the gravel in the unplanted squares. Even if these were left empty, the design would be attractive and could be extended to form a border to a path. In this short band a summer display is made of potted standards of the calamondin (× *Citrofortunella microcarpa*). Many other potted plants could be used instead, in a seasonal succession.

3 *Enclosed cross*
This design, which consists of a modified square of cotton lavender, is approximately 6½ft (2m) square. The cross is in effect a square within a square, its arms being what remains after a circular bite has been taken out of each side. The circular holes could hold potted plants but the cotton lavender will certainly suffer if it is shaded for long periods.

4 *Interweaving scrolls*
The scroll-like designs that displaced the severe geometry of traditional knot gardens were usually executed on a grand scale. The simplicity of this fluid design for a rectangular bed about 20ft (6m) by 13ft (4m) is a happy compromise. The pattern is symmetrical and interweaving, as in a knot garden, but open and elegantly scroll-like, as in an embroidered parterre. The border and pattern are planted in dwarf boxwood. The interweaving scrolls are meant to stand out against a background of long-flowering bedding plants such as annual semperflorens begonias.

5 *Square check pattern*
Here a square is divided into nine equal compartments by a grid of bricks, which are also used for the surround. Each compartment is 24in (60cm) square and the total length of a side is 6ft (1.8m), so this pattern could make the centerpiece of a small garden. The compartments running diagonally are planted with boxwood triangles; the center square on each side is planted with cotton lavender. The plants are surrounded by a gravel mulch. There are rich possibilities for variations or multiplication to make a pair or foursome.

An Art Deco garden

The eclectic international Art Deco style, although making a strong mark in many fields of design during its heyday in the 1920s and 1930s, had little impact on the layout of gardens. Perhaps it seemed too associated with mass production. However, the inventive and playful use of geometric patterns makes the Art Deco style a fertile source of ideas for formal gardens that are not set in the Renaissance mold.

The small gardens that are among the delightful details of old topographical illustrations have influenced the design for the town garden shown opposite. Its urban location provides prime positions—the upper storeys of buildings—from which to view the pattern. The rectangle, approximately 40ft (12m) long by 20ft (6m) wide, could be dropped into a narrow walled garden, a path running around on all four sides. In a longer garden there might be room for an area with tables and chairs at one end. In a smaller garden the border, its angled gaps filled with cones, and the cornerpieces, consisting of one drum superimposed upon another, could be omitted, leaving the central design contained by its brick edging in a bed of gravel. The design could also be used as a component in a larger scheme, ideally one where terracing or a raised walk allowed the pattern to be seen clearly from an elevated position.

The play of light and shade in this strongly rhythmic design is dramatically enhanced by elaborating the pattern in three planes with variations in height. The three squares, ranged in line but touching only at a corner, are each composed of three parallel hedges, the two broad outer ones 32in (80cm) wide and 16in (40cm) high. The total length of a side is 8½ft (2.6m). The inner hedge, only 8in (20cm) wide but 24in (60cm) high, is matched by the curved hedges that bind the squares together. This pattern would work quite happily with no planting between the hedges. The less severe approach adopted here fills the gaps with seasonal flowers. The garden is seen in spring, the narrow beds planted with red and yellow tulips.

LEFT Swastika-like patterns lock into a larger scheme composed of close hedges of boxwood, which are clipped to a uniform height, except for low finials and outcrops of pyramids.

N

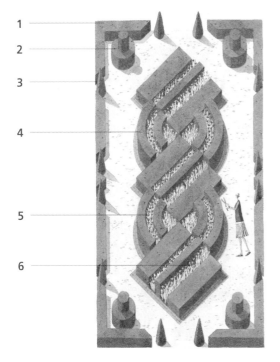

1 Boxwood hedge surrounding an
   Art Deco pattern on four sides
   but broken at points of entry
   and to accommodate cones
2 1 of 4 topiary shapes in boxwood,
   each consisting of a small drum
   superimposed on a larger one
3 1 of 12 boxwood cones
4 Art Deco pattern consisting of
   interlocking curved and straight
   hedges in boxwood
5 Red-flowered tulips
6 Yellow-flowered tulips

Approximately 40ft (12m) by 20ft (6m)

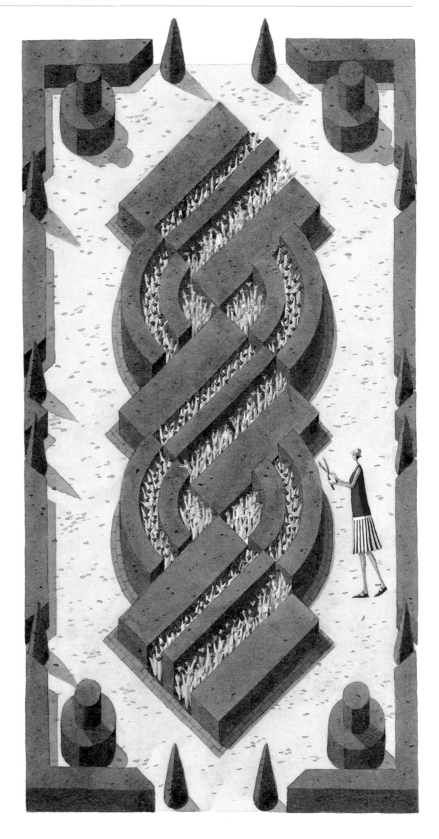

Simple beds and compartments

What is called a knot garden is more often than not simply a number of boxwood-edged beds arranged in a pleasing pattern. Simple beds, outlined in a dwarf hedging plant such as boxwood, may seem unadventurous in comparison with the patterned complexities of over-and-under knot designs or embroidered parterres, but their no-nonsense tidiness is their virtue. When beds are full of flowers, they make an unobtrusive but neat green trim. In winter their sober order has its own appeal. It is perhaps then that their arrangement in patterns is most easily appreciated.

In the 17th century the beds might have contained no more than a colored ground or mown grass, the pattern being the garden's ornament. Squares, rectangles and circles predominated but more complex shapes, often scalloped, were much used. The same was true in the 19th century, when garden designers, looking back to the 17th century, laid out schemes that were a jigsaw puzzle of variously shaped geometric beds, usually arranged in tight symmetry. To the modern eye some of the layouts may seem fussy, even though their re-creation is of historical interest. Straightforward layouts of squares and rectangles are not burdened by historical associations and readily adapt to gardens of different character and size. In the larger garden they make a pleasing contrast to the looser planting of mixed and herbaceous borders, in which some disorder in the ranks and breaking of the line helps create the impression of a spontaneous assembly.

There are many ways the modern gardener can approach the planting of boxwood-edged beds. You could make a nostalgic reference to old gardens with herbs and other plants known to have been grown in the 16th and 17th centuries. *Plates-bandes*, the boxwood-edged beds surrounding embroidered parterres, were planted rather sparsely, with rarities, such as highly prized tulips, being displayed as though the garden were an outdoor cabinet of curiosities. Nineteenth-century gardeners, delighting in the numerous new introductions and equipped with glasshouses that made large-scale propagation feasible, created vibrant color schemes with a gusto that can make the "good taste" of the 20th century sometimes seem pallid. It is a matter of individual judgment as to what plants and what color schemes are used but a particularly satisfying and restrained combination, authentically 17th-century but curiously modern in feel, consists of an ordered planting of cotton lavender within boxwood hedges, these perhaps punctuated by a few boxwood cones. The cotton lavender plants, clipped annually in spring, form gray blocks, but the individual plants retain enough of their shape to create the impression of a lightly upholstered cushion.

LEFT A richly planted garden uses the adaptable formula of rectilinear beds outlined in low hedges and an arbor with trained roses along a main axis.

OPPOSITE In the Jardin Potager at Villandry in France, the small beds bursting with vegetables give an idea of how this form of patterning was used on a large scale in 16th-century French gardens.

ABOVE Flowing lines of lavender, cotton lavender and a dwarf purple-leaved *Berberis thunbergii* make a relaxed over-and-under pattern that seems on the point of melting away.

LEFT A gray crisscross pattern of cotton lavender forms small compartments planted sparsely with tulips for a spring display. The style harks back to the 16th century. The now familiar massed planting of bulbs and summer bedding developed in the 19th century.

OPPOSITE In a view that isolates them from the overall pattern, shapes in trimmed boxwood seem like fragments of an archipelago marooned in a sea of lavender.

Mazes

The complexity of the Cretan labyrinth is the stuff of nightmares. In the classical myth, once the Athenian youths and maidens delivered to King Minos as tribute had been given up to the Minotaur, a savage flesh-eating man-beast, there was virtually no chance of escape from the intricate network of passageways. Theseus could retrace his steps after slaying the monster only because of the thread that he had played out on entering. The labyrinth, however, has many guises. Sometimes it is charged with a magical or religious significance. In the garden the best-known version is the hedge maze, where the twists and turns of the paths, some of which are dead ends, are confusing but have the innocent intention of providing harmless entertainment. One should, however, beware of the false confidence of Harris in Jerome K. Jerome's novel *Three Men in a Boat*, when he volunteered to conduct a party around the Hampton Court maze: "It's absurd to call it a maze. You keep on taking the first turning to the right. We'll just walk round for ten minutes and then go and get some lunch."

Hedge mazes

Most of the surviving and re-created historic hedge mazes are of the kind that was popular in the 17th century, when the general taste favored complex geometric designs. These mazes, usually laid out in a square, rectangle or circle (that at Hampton Court is trapezoid in shape), consist of a close network of paths separated from each other by head-high hedges. As an entertainment the success of the design depends on devising a route to the center, perhaps marked by a mount or small pavilion, that is intricate enough to cause bewilderment without creating panic. As an ornamental feature a hedge maze is fully appreciated only if it can be viewed from a vantage point, such as a raised terrace or the windows of a building. There may be pleasure in observing the faltering progress of the maze's visitors but the enduring visual interest of the maze lies in its pattern and the tide-like movement of shadows in its depths.

The delights of a hedge maze are best enjoyed in the context

The yew maze at Chatsworth in Derbyshire was planted in 1963, more than 250 years after the most famous maze in England, that at Hampton Court, was originally laid out. Enjoying the shifting play of light and shade on Chatsworth's maze is an agreeable alternative to finding a way through its twists and turns.

of a large garden. Mature hedges of yew, the ideal planting material, will be about 24in (60cm) wide and a path between them could not be much under 30in (75cm) wide; so when assessing a site for suitability you need to base calculations on approximately 4½ft (1.4m) between the hedges' planting lines. Even a simplified maze cannot be much under 40ft (12m) across. This may not seem impossible for a moderate-sized garden but a maze is so dominant that it will overwhelm all but the largest gardens.

Apart from scale, another point to bear in mind is the labor involved in its maintenance. A calculation of hedge and path lengths can add up to sobering totals. The hedges need regular trimming and the paths must be kept in good condition. Grassed paths must be cut frequently and in any case do not wear well, especially if there is traffic when they are wet. A firm well-drained gravel path is the ideal, but shredded bark is pleasant underfoot and a path surfaced with it, provided the base is well drained, requires little maintenance.

In laying out a hedge maze it is essential to select a well-drained site in an open position. On heavy and poorly drained soils traffic concentrated on the paths can cause compaction, leading to poor growth and even the death of hedge plants; yew and boxwood are especially susceptible to poor drainage. The long life that can be expected of a maze warrants taking trouble to prepare the ground, by digging it thoroughly, removing perennial weeds and working in copious quantities of organic matter. The ground must be allowed to settle for two or three months before planting.

As with knots and embroidered parterres, the layout should be drawn to scale on graph paper. Transfer the outer edge of the design to the ground first, by marking a base line that, depending on the shape of the design, is the required length of the diameter of a circle or one side of a square or rectangle. In the case of a circle, swing a tape in an arc from the center of the base line at the length of the required radius, and mark the circumference in dry sand dribbled from a bottle. In the case of a square or rectangle, there are various ways of measuring right angles, using geometric principles or improvising with a shape you know to be right-angled.

With the outer hedge line marked on the ground, the inside hedge lines can be marked on the ground in relation to it. Straight lines should be marked out using garden line but curves measured from the center using a tape swinging in an arc at the required length are most easily marked out in dry sand. Once you have transferred the design of the maze to the ground, you can plant it in the same way as an ordinary hedge.

The most tiresome pest of the hedge maze is the rambunctious child, who, quickly tiring of the puzzle, impatiently pushes through from one path to another. One can regret that there is no Minotaur slavering for tribute! If you cannot exclude children from a maze until the hedges have thickened, it is worth erecting netting along the paths so that it is impossible to make shortcuts.

Other mazes

An interesting alternative to the hedge maze, which requires no clipping other than the mowing of grass, is the turf maze. This is a revival of a medieval type with symbolic or religious significance. The path of the turf maze does not usually offer choices but its tight winding passage suggests a pilgrimage or ritualistic dance. Turf mazes are normally paved, but can be given the magical character of a crop circle by cutting grass according to different mowing regimes, so that short-mown paths wind through a hay crop of tall grass, mixed perhaps with wild flowers. Like the hedge maze, the turf maze requires plenty of space.

In small gardens the best way of creating the mysterious feeling of a maze is to divide the space into small compartments and to arrange hedges, shrubs or beds to make a circuitous passage through the garden, as in the second compartment of the garden illustrated on page 69. Provided there is a vantage point from which it can be seen, a maze-like pattern without paths can be effectively laid out as flowerbeds or low hedges. A less rigorous approach than that followed in Renaissance gardens would allow many other interesting designs—more patterns than puzzles—to be tried. For instance, in Asian mode a stylized version of the Chinese character *shou*, frequently used as a decoration representing good fortune, would make a splendid pattern in boxwood; so too would the Yin-Yang symbol surrounded by the eight trigrams, with all the possible variants of a long line (Yang) and two short lines (Yin) arranged in groups of three.

Directory

Plants listed in the Directory are given a hardiness rating.
FULLY HARDY withstanding temperatures down to 5°F (–15°C)
FROST HARDY withstanding temperatures down to 23°F (–5°C)
HALF-HARDY withstanding temperatures down to 32°F (0°C)
FROST TENDER these plants are given the minimum temperature at which they can normally be grown, e.g. min. 41°F (5°C)
See map on page 156 for regional average annual minimum temperatures in the U.S. and Canada.

PLANTS FOR TOPIARY AND HEDGES

The following selection of shrubs and trees covers those widely used for topiary and formal hedges in formal gardens, although it is not intended to be comprehensive. A brief introduction to each genus is followed by a selection of species and cultivars. For each species, its place of origin is described (no region is given for hybrids of garden origin), followed by its hardiness. The information given here is tailored to the cultivation of the plants as clipped shapes but many also have other ornamental uses; likewise the information given on propagation is that most appropriate for raising plants for topiary and hedges. For treatment of the pests and diseases listed as problems, see page 16.

ARTEMISIA

The best-known of several hundred species are a number of aromatic shrubby plants of dry habitats. Of these, southernwood responds best to trimming and has long been used as an edging plant or as a low hedge in knot gardens.
A. abrotanum Lad's love, old man, southernwood
S. Europe. FULLY HARDY.
In sunny well-drained conditions plants make mounds 40in (1m) high of feathery sage-green leaves, which are

pleasantly aromatic. When trimmed regularly to about 18in (45cm) the yellow button flowers are sacrificed.
PLANTING/SPACING In early to mid-fall or in early to mid-spring. 1ft (30cm).
MAINTENANCE Clip annually in early spring and then two or three times in summer.
PROPAGATION From semi-ripe cuttings in mid-summer.
PROBLEMS Usually none.

BUXUS BOXWOOD

Of the species in this genus of evergreen shrubs and trees, the common boxwood is the first choice for small-scale topiary and is widely used for low to medium-size hedges or, in its dwarf forms, for edging. Although there are about seventy other species, only a few are much used in gardens. The most frequently seen after the common boxwood is *B. microphylla*, the small-leaved boxwood. There are very hardy forms, some dwarf and slow-growing.
'**Green Pillow,**' makes a dense hummock with no clipping.
B. sempervirens Common boxwood
Europe, N. Africa, Turkey.
FULLY HARDY.
The common boxwood is a bushy shrub or small tree that is well covered with dark green glossy leaves. It thrives on a wide range of well-drained soils, including alkaline, and tolerates light shade. Its advantages as a topiary and hedging plant, recognized since Roman times, are that it develops a dense surface when regularly clipped and is relatively slow-growing, and so it retains its shape well with only one trim a year. The vigor and erect growth of '**Handsworthiensis**' make it the best choice for taller hedges and topiary, say 5–8ft (1.5–2.5m) high, although it can be trained to over 10ft (3m). The variegated boxwoods tend to revert when regularly clipped. The best of the silver boxwoods is '**Elegantissima,**' with dense foliage, the small leaves edged creamy white. In '**Notata,**' widely sold but often unnamed, the top leaves have a yellow tip. The indispensable cultivar for edging and low patterns is '**Suffruticosa,**' which will grow to over 4ft (1.2m) but can be kept to 6in (15cm). '**Latifolia

Maculata**' is also dwarf but its leaves are larger than those of 'Suffruticosa' and blotched yellow.
PLANTING/SPACING In early fall or early to mid-spring. 12–16in (30–40cm), dwarf box 6in (15cm).
MAINTENANCE For a scrupulous finish, clip twice annually in summer, otherwise once in late summer. To renovate, prune in early spring.
PROPAGATION From semi-ripe cuttings in summer and early fall.
PROBLEMS Boxwood leaf miner, red spider mite; canker, leaf spot.

CARPINUS HORNBEAM

There are approximately forty species of hornbeam, all deciduous trees of the temperate northern hemisphere. The common hornbeam is a hedging plant of exceptional quality but another species that can be used in a similar way is *C. caroliniana*, the American hornbeam, a less vigorous tree but with brighter foliage.
C. betulus European hornbeam
Europe, Asia Minor.
FULLY HARDY.
In the past, common hornbeam was frequently coppiced or pollarded to provide firewood and has been much used for tall hedges where gardens have been laid out in the French grand manner. Common hornbeam is a versatile hedging plant for the modern garden, thriving in a wide range of soils provided drainage is good, and responding to clipping by forming a dense surface of almost oval leaves that are mid-green, serrated and deeply veined. Plants that are clipped retain their dead leaves until spring. Common hornbeam can be trained to make a hedge from 5ft (1.5m) to over 20ft (6m) high, and when grown as an aerial hedge or as trimmed blocks of foliage on clear stems the beauty of the gray, often fluted trunks can be appreciated. Young growth is flexible, allowing hornbeam to be pleached or trained on frames to form tunnels. The catkins and winged nutlets are lost with regular trimming.

PLANTING/SPACING From fall to early spring. Hedges: 24in (60cm); aerial hedges and pleached hornbeam: 6–13ft (2–4m).

MAINTENANCE Clip once annually in summer. Carry out major pruning in winter, when plants are dormant. Avoid pruning in spring, when wounds are likely to bleed heavily.
PROPAGATION From seed sown in fall; from greenwood cuttings in early summer.
PROBLEMS Aphids, caterpillars; leaf miner.

CHAMAECYPARIS
FALSE CYPRESS

The foliage in this small genus of evergreen conifers is arranged in flattened sprays, a feature that helps to distinguish them from the related true cypresses of the genus *Cupressus*. The species have produced numerous sports, some of which are naturally compact and slow-growing.
C. lawsoniana Lawson cypress
North America. FULLY HARDY.
On deep soils where there is plenty of moisture, specimens develop into tall columns, usually of somber green, although the color is very variable. Some cultivars, particularly *C.l.* '**Kilmacurragh,**' develop narrow spires, similar to those of *Cupressus sempervirens* 'Stricta,' the Italian cypress. The Lawson cypress makes a vigorous hedging plant that can be grown to a height of 10–15ft (3–4.5m), forming an effective windbreak in exposed positions. The pick of the tall-growing cultivars is *C.l.* '**Green Hedger,**' with rich green dense foliage to the base. The compact, slower-growing *C.l.* '**Fletcheri,**' with feathery, gray-green foliage, makes a hedge up to about 8ft (2.5m) high.

PLANTING/SPACING Early fall or mid- to late spring. 18–24in (45–60cm).
MAINTENANCE Trim twice annually, in early summer and early fall.
PROPAGATION From semi-ripe cuttings in mid- to late summer.
PROBLEMS Aphids; *Phytophthora* root rot.

CRATAEGUS HAWTHORN

The hawthorns, of which there are about 200 species widely distributed in northern temperate regions, are tough and usually spiny deciduous or semi-evergreen shrubs and trees. Several European species that are tough and versatile and easily propagated have long been used as farm hedges that are effective stock barriers.

C. monogyna Single-leaved hawthorn
Europe.
FULLY HARDY.
Common hawthorn is a standard constituent of the agricultural laid hedge (see p. 88). In its own right it makes ornamental hedges of great character, although not achieving absolute precision. Hedges are best shaped with a rounded top. Regular clipping means that a high proportion of the white flowers and red fruits are lost. Although not suitable for crisp topiary shapes, hawthorn looks very handsome when trimmed to form a dome. Other hawthorns that can be trained and shaped in the same way as the common hawthorn include another European species, *C. laevigata*.

PLANTING/SPACING Between mid-fall and late winter. 12–18in (30–45cm).
MAINTENANCE Clip twice annually, in early summer after flowering, and in fall after leaf fall.
PROPAGATION From seed, in early winter (germination may take 18 months).
PROBLEMS Caterpillars, scab; fireblight, rust, powdery mildew.

x CUPRESSOCYPARIS
This hybrid genus of vigorous evergreen conifers, the result of crosses between *Chamaecyparis* and *Cupressus*, includes several distinctive columnar trees with foliage in flattened sprays.
x C. leylandii Leyland cypress
FULLY HARDY.
The vigor of this bigeneric cross makes it useful as a windbreak, planted in a staggered line and widely spaced. It is much used for hedges that are 10ft (3m) or more high, often inappropriately, for its vigor counts against it as a hedging plant. Avoid it except as a short-term measure to shelter other hedges while they are still young, or to create standards or simple shapes. The usual foliage color is green to gray-green. **'Haggerston Grey'** has gray-green foliage. The less

vigorous **'Castlewellan'** is sulfurous bronze.

PLANTING/SPACING In mid- to late spring. 18–24in (45–60cm).
MAINTENANCE Trim two or three times a year between early summer and early fall.
PROPAGATION From semi-ripe cuttings in late summer.
PROBLEMS Bag worm.

CUPRESSUS CYPRESS
The 20 or so species of cypress are evergreen conifers of the northern hemisphere. Several have been much used for hedges and topiary, the Italian cypress in particular being associated with formal gardens dominated by green architecture. All tolerate a wide range of soils provided they are well drained but the lack of hardiness of many of these conifers limits their usefulness in cool temperate regions.
C. arizonica **var. *glabra***
Smooth cypress
S.W. U.S.A.
FROST HARDY TO FULLY HARDY.
The purplish bark gives the smooth cypress its common name but it is the dense blue-gray foliage that makes it an impressive hedging plant, which can be trained to a height of about 10ft (3m). The relative hardiness of this species makes it particularly useful.
C. macrocarpa Monterey cypress
California, U.S.A.
FROST HARDY TO FULLY HARDY.
The Monterey cypress, which has a very restricted natural distribution in California, has been much used as a fast-growing hedge in coastal areas. Hedges can be trained to more than 13ft (4m) but they tend to lose their shape when mature and become bare at the base. As topiary the Monterey cypress is best used for uncomplicated shapes, such as drums. Golden-leaved forms include **'Donard Gold'** and **'Goldcrest,'** which is a compact and columnar form.
C. sempervirens Italian cypress, Mediterranean cypress
Mediterranean east to Iran.
FROST HARDY TO FULLY HARDY.
The dark green narrow columnar forms are strongly associated with the Italian landscape but forms of more

spreading growth have been much used for hedges and large-scale topiary. Where this species is grown at the margins of its hardiness it is young plants that are most vulnerable. John Evelyn, the 17th-century diarist and enormously influential writer on trees, was enthusiastic about the tree in England but almost all the specimens then growing were killed in the severe winter of 1683–84.

PLANTING/SPACING In early to late spring. 18–24in (45–60cm).
MAINTENANCE Clip once annually in late spring or early summer.
PROPAGATION From semi-ripe cuttings in late summer; from seed in spring.
PROBLEMS Canker.

FAGUS BEECH
The beeches, of which there are 10 species, are forest trees of the temperate northern hemisphere. Only one is generally used for hedging; but although it is used widely, it is often a source of surprise that such a splendid large tree should also make one of the best deciduous hedging plants.
F. grandifolia, the American beech, can also be trained; it has been used, for instance, to form a tunnel in the lower garden of the Governor's Palace at Colonial Williamsburg, Virginia.
F. sylvatica European beech
Europe. FULLY HARDY.
The common beech is a versatile hedging plant that thrives on a wide range of well-drained soils, acid and alkaline, and is tolerant of light shade. It is easily trained to make hedges 6–20ft (1.8–6m) high. Although deciduous, when regularly trimmed it retains its dead leaves through winter, giving a superb seasonal sequence from bright green to glossy deep green and then to yellow and copper. It is only for a short season that there is no foliage screen. Copper- and purple-leaved beeches such as **'Riversii'** make a very dark and somber enclosure, and are seen at their best contrasted with plain-leaved beech in a mixed hedge.

PLANTING/SPACING From mid-fall to early spring. 18–24in (45–60cm).
MAINTENANCE Trim once or twice annually in summer.

PROPAGATION From seed, sown outdoors in fall; by grafting.
PROBLEMS Scale insects, especially beech bark scale; beech bark disease, bracket fungi.

ILEX HOLLY
The best-known hollies are evergreens with colorful berries in winter clustered among leaves that are usually to some extent spined. The classic hollies for hedging and topiary conform to this model, although cultivars without spines, which produce leaf litter almost free of prickles, are preferable for the most heavily worked areas of the garden. There is, however, great variety in a genus of several hundred species of deciduous and evergreen shrubs and trees (even some climbers) that are widely distributed in temperate and tropical regions. Male and female flowers are usually borne on separate plants, and female plants need a male plant close by to produce berries. The hollies listed here, all evergreen, thrive in sun or light shade in moist well-drained conditions, but also do well in light soils and are suitable for coastal gardens.
I. x *altaclerensis*
FROST HARDY TO FULLY HARDY.
The hybrids that go under this name are similar in appearance to one of the parents, the English holly. Most of these large-leaved and vigorous evergreen shrubs or trees make excellent hedges to a height of 10ft (3m) or more and are also suitable for simple topiary shapes. The berries are red. **'Camelliifolia'** is female with deep green, almost spineless leaves on purplish stems. **'Golden King,'** female despite its name, has leaves with few or no spines, green or mottled in the center and with a yellow irregular edge. The vigorous **'Hodginsii'** is male with very dark green, variably spined leaves on purplish stems.
I. aquifolium English holly
Europe, N. Africa, W. Asia.
FULLY HARDY.
This glossy-leaved large shrub or tree is very variable: the numerous forms have spined or spineless leaves and many selections are handsomely variegated. The berries are usually red but in some forms they are yellow.

Many cultivars make fine hedges 15ft (4.5m) or more in height and are also suitable for uncomplicated topiary shapes. '**Argentea Marginata**,' male and female, has spiny leaves with silvery variegation, although when young they are purplish pink. '**Ferox**,' the hedgehog holly, is male and its small leaves are congested with short spines. It is relatively slow-growing but makes a formidable barrier 6½– 8ft (2–2.5m) high. There are also variegated forms of it. '**J.C. van Tol**,' female and capable of berrying prolifically, has dark green, almost spineless leaves. '**Golden Queen**,' a perversely named male clone, has broad spiny leaves with a dark green and mottled center and bright yellow margin.

I. crenata Box-leaved holly, Japanese holly
Korea, Japan, Sakhalin Is.
FULLY HARDY.
The small, shiny, mid-green leaves have a lightly scalloped margin and the berries of this slow-growing holly are black. '**Convexa**,' which is female and berries prolifically, lives up to the description "boxwood-leaved" and makes a dense hedge 4–6½ft (1.2–2m) high.

I. opaca American holly
C. and E. US.A. FULLY HARDY
In parts of America this is the most widely grown holly, making hedges 10ft (3m) or more high, but it does not tolerate chalky soils. It is used, for example, in the maze at the Governor's Palace, Colonial Williamsburg, Virginia. The leaves are leathery and matt, mid- to olive-green and sparsely spined. The berries are usually crimson but there are cultivars with yellow and orange fruit.

I. vomitoria Yaupon
S.E. U.S.A. Mexico.
HALF-HARDY.
In the southern United States, as in the gardens at Colonial Williamsburg, Virginia, this glossy-leaved holly is used as an alternative to boxwood for low hedges and small-scale topiary. The berries are bright red or, in some cultivars, yellow.

PLANTING/SPACING In early fall or mid- to late spring. 18–24in (45–60cm).
MAINTENANCE Clip in mid- to late summer. To renovate, cut back in early spring, staging the operation over two to three years.
PROPAGATION From semi-ripe cuttings in late summer.
PROBLEMS Leaf miners, scale insects; *Phytophthora* root rot.

JUNIPERUS JUNIPER
There are 50 or so species in this genus of evergreen conifers, which are widely distributed in the northern hemisphere. This total is supplemented by a large number of cultivars. The juvenile foliage is needle-like but in most species adult leaves are scale-like. Junipers usually need little pruning, the growth of trees and the numerous slow-growing dwarf forms being dense, and in some cases strikingly regular. *J. chinensis*, the Chinese juniper, is a favorite plant for cloud pruning, and in the past the common juniper was much used for topiary and hedging.

J. communis Common juniper
N. hemisphere.
FULLY HARDY.
The astonishing distribution of this tough shrub or small tree indicates its tolerance of a wide range of conditions, including thin soils on chalk. The foliage remains needle-like even on mature plants. Columnar forms such as '**Hibernica**,' the Irish juniper, which makes a narrow spire 10–16ft (3–5m) high, and '**Compressa**,' rarely much more than 32in (80cm) high, are so regular and compact that they need no trimming to achieve a formal shape. 'Hibernica' can be used for a narrow gray-blue hedge to a height of about 6½ft (2m). When grown as topiary, the common juniper is best shaped as a simple ball on a stem.

PLANTING/SPACING In mid-spring. 18in (45cm).
MAINTENANCE Clip once annually in summer.
PROPAGATION From ripewood cuttings in early fall.
PROBLEMS Aphids, scale insects; rust.

LAURUS BAY LAUREL
There are only two species in the genus, both aromatic evergreens. The bay laurel is an indispensable culinary herb and highly ornamental as a shaped specimen.

L. nobilis Bay laurel *Mediterranean region.* FROST HARDY.
The sweet bay is a plant for full sun and well-drained soil. In a favorable climate it can develop into a tree well over 33ft (10m) in height and even when grown as a hedge in coastal areas of temperate regions it can easily top 20ft (6m). The leaves are too large for detailed clipping but the sweet bay has long been a favorite for trimming as topiary balls, domes, obelisks and pyramids. The stems of mopheads are sometimes trained with a baroque twist. In frost-prone areas the bay laurel is best grown in a container and moved under cover from late fall to early spring.

PLANTING/SPACING In early to mid-spring. 24in (60cm).
MAINTENANCE Trim to shape one to three times a year between early summer and early fall, removing whole leaves or clusters of leaves with secateurs.
PROPAGATION From semi-ripe cuttings in late summer or early fall.
PROBLEMS Bay sucker, scale insect.

LAVANDULA LAVENDER
The lavenders are evergreen shrubs or subshrubs with aromatic foliage and fragrant flowers. Approximately 25 species are distributed from the Canary Islands across southern Europe and North Africa as far as India. The Mediterranean species have long been cultivated for their flowers and also as low hedges and edging. None grows much above 3ft (90cm) and more compact lavenders are 20–30in (50–75cm) high. All lavenders, which are tolerant of lime, need full sun and well-drained soil. With an annual trim in spring they remain reasonably compact and the flower display is not sacrificed; it is better to follow this clipping regime, using them as informal hedges or edging, rather than trimming more frequently for a more formal effect, which results in fewer or no flowers. Plants gradually become leggy and are best replaced after five years. Where the climate is mild enough, some of the more tender species, including *L. lanata*, with leaves that are wooly and almost white, can be substituted for the more familiar lavenders.

L. angustifolia Common or English lavender
Mediterranean. FULLY HARDY.
The numerous cultivars of this narrow-leaved species show differences in vigor and flower color. '**Hidcote**,' about 24in (60cm) high, with dark purple flowers, is one of the most popular. '**Loddon Pink**,' slightly more compact, provides a useful color variation. '**Nana Alba**,' white-flowered and only about 12in (30cm) high, is suitable for edging.

L. x intermedia Lavandin
FROST HARDY TO FULLY HARDY.
Crosses between *L. angustifolia* and another Mediterranean species, *L. latifolia*, have produced a range of lavenders with gray-green leaves that are linear to nearly spoon-shaped and flower spikes that are light blue to purplish violet. **Dutch Group**, Dutch lavender, has a more silvery and broader leaf than **Old English Group**, Old English lavender, hearty silvery-gray plants with pale flowers. '**Grappenhall**,' which can have a spread of up to 5ft (1.5m), is one of the most substantial lavenders for a hedge and has purplish blue flowers.

L. stoechas French lavender
Mediterranean. FROST TO FULLY HARDY.
In warm dry conditions the French lavender, which grows to 24in (60cm), is suitable for an informal hedge or edging. It is well worth retaining the curious display of dark purple flower spikes topped by purple bracts.

PLANTING/SPACING In early fall or early spring. 10–12in (25–30cm).
MAINTENANCE Clip annually in early to mid-spring and trim lightly in late summer.
PROPAGATION From semi-ripe cuttings in summer.
PROBLEMS Froghoppers (which produce cuckoo spit); gray mold.

LIGUSTRUM PRIVET
There are about 50 species of privet, some of which make fast-growing hedges. Those listed here are tolerant of a wide range of soils and will grow in shade. *L. lucidum*, the wax leaf

privet, is a large evergreen shrub or small tree with glossy pointed leaves which, left untrimmed, produces large heads of white flowers in late summer. *L. lucidum* and the striking yellow variegated **L. l. 'Excelsum Superbum'** can be trained to make handsome dome-headed standards up to 10ft (3m) high.

L. delavayanum

W. China. FULLY HARDY.
The relatively fast growth, small glossy leaves and pliant stems of this evergreen species make it popular with nurseries for training shapes on frames. It is suitable for a hedge to about 5ft (1.5m).

L. japonicum Japanese privet

N. China, Japan, Korea. FULLY HARDY.
The glossy dark-green leaves of this evergreen make it an attractive standard or hedge when grown to a height of about 6½ft (2m). The white flowers are borne in late summer.

L. ovalifolium California privet

Japan. FULLY HARDY.
When left unpruned, this evergreen or semi-evergreen shrub can grow to 16ft (5m) or more but as a hedge, as it is most commonly grown, it is usually kept to a maximum of 10ft (3m). It is a greedy feeder and requires several trims a year but is a useful fast-growing hedge, all the better when clipping removes the flowers, which have an unpleasant smell. It is sometimes used for light-hearted topiary but detail is quickly lost if trimming is neglected. **'Argenteum,'** with cool white variegation, and **'Aureum,'** the golden privet, are useful accents as clipped shapes.

PLANTING/SPACING In fall or early to mid-spring. 12–18in (30–45cm).
MAINTENANCE Trim at least twice annually, in early and late summer.
PROPAGATION From semi-ripe cuttings in summer or hardwood cuttings in fall.
PROBLEMS Aphids, scale insects; anthracnose, leaf spot.

LONICERA HONEYSUCKLE

The climbing honeysuckles grab the limelight but among nearly 200 species there are a number of deciduous and evergreen shrubs of horticultural value.

L. nitida Boxleaf honeysuckle

China. FULLY HARDY.
Left untrimmed this fast-growing evergreen shrub will reach 6ft (1.8m) but as a hedge it is usually kept to about 4ft (1.2m). It is also used for simple topiary shapes. Bushes are densely covered in boxwood-like leaves that are glossy dark green but remain compact only if trimmed several times a year. It tolerates a wide range of soil conditions and does well in shade. **'Baggesen's Gold,'** often planted for the sunniness of its yellow foliage in spring and early summer, can look more sickly than cheerful. In shade it is a light green.

PLANTING/SPACING In mid- to late spring. 10–12in (25–30cm).
MAINTENANCE Trim at least twice annually, in early summer and early fall.
PROPAGATION From semi–ripe cuttings in summer.
PROBLEMS Usually none.

MYRTUS MYRTLE

Changes in botanical classification have left only one species of horticultural importance in the genus. The common myrtle has long been cultivated and has a happy association with love and marriage: sprigs were once included in wedding bouquets.

M. communis Common myrtle

Mediterranean. FROST HARDY.
The myrtle is an evergreen shrub with small dark green leaves that are richly aromatic. In a warm garden it will thrive in a sunny position on free-draining soil, producing fragrant white flowers in late summer, which are followed by small dark purple berries. It is sometimes grown as an informal hedge, lightly trimmed after flowering and usually kept below 8ft (2.5m). With more severe trimming, which inevitably sacrifices most of the floral display, it can make a formal hedge or simple topiary shapes. **Subsp. *tarentina*,** the Tarentin myrtle, is small-leaved and compact.

PLANTING/SPACING In mid- to late spring. 18–24in (45–60cm).
MAINTENANCE For formal hedges clip twice annually, in early and late summer.

PROPAGATION From semi-ripe cuttings in late summer.
PROBLEMS Usually none.

PHILLYREA

The evergreen shrubs and trees of this small genus are rather neglected as ornamentals, but in the 17th century *P. angustifolia* was much used for topiary and its dense growth suits this purpose and hedging well.

P. angustifolia

Mediterranean. FULLY HARDY.
For topiary and hedges this shrub is best grown in a reasonably sheltered sunny position where the soil is fertile but well drained. Clipping encourages the dense growth of narrow dark green leaves but the relatively slow growth rate means that hedges and topiary are rarely much more than 6ft (1.8m) high. Even slower-growing is the fine-leaved **f. *rosmarinifolia*.** The flowers are greenish white and inconspicuous but sweetly fragrant. Inevitably clipped plants produce far fewer flowers than free-growing specimens.

PLANTING/SPACING In mid- to late spring. 45cm/18in.
MAINTENANCE Trim annually in early summer after flowering, and, ideally, again in late summer.
PROPAGATION Semi-ripe cuttings with bottom heat in summer or early fall; layering in spring.
PROBLEMS Usually none.

PITTOSPORUM

The genus, consisting of about 200 species of mainly evergreen shrubs and trees, is strongly represented in Australasia. Several species are widely used there for hedging and do well in other regions where the climate is mild enough. Those described thrive in open positions where the soil is moist but well drained and are particularly useful in coastal conditions.

P. crassifolium Karo

New Zealand. HALF-HARDY.
Leathery leaves, dark green on the upper surface, buff on the underside, make a dense protective hedge 8–10ft (2.5–3m) high that is ideal for seaside gardens where the climate is mild enough.

P. tenuifolium Kohuhu

New Zealand. FROST HARDY.
The untrimmed plant is beautiful on account of the contrast between the nearly black stems and the glossy pale green leaves, which have a markedly wavy edge. However, it makes an excellent hedge to about 10ft (3m) in mild areas and some of the forms with variegated, gold or purple leaves (not usually as hardy as the type) are suitable for smaller hedges. The kohuhu can also be trimmed to make simple topiary shapes.

PLANTING/SPACING In mid- to late spring. 18in (45cm).
MAINTENANCE Trim annually in mid- to late spring and mid-summer.
PROPAGATION From semi-ripe cuttings in mid-summer.
PROBLEMS Usually none.

PRUNUS

This large and horticulturally important genus of more than 200 species includes the evergreen cherry laurels as well as several deciduous trees that are suitable for hedging.

P. cerasifera Cherry plum, myrobalan

S.E. Europe, Asia Minor. FULLY HARDY.
Left untrimmed, this deciduous species grows to 20ft (6m) or more, its stems covered with small white flowers in early spring, which are sometimes followed by small red cherry plums. With regular trimming it makes a dense twiggy hedge 5–8ft (1.5–2.5m) high and is suitable for open positions on most well-drained soils. **'Nigra'** and **'Pissardii'** are purple-leaved cultivars much used for hedging but somber in the height of summer.

P. x cistena, a purple-leaved hybrid, is slow-growing and useful for hedges up to 5ft (1.5m) high.

P. incisa Fuji cherry

Japan. FULLY HARDY.
This species is more shrubby than the cherry plum but makes a hedge to a height of 6½ft (2m). As a result of trimming, the pink-tinted floral display of early spring or, in the case of **'Praecox,'** of late winter, is reduced. A striking feature, even of shaped plants, is the rich coloring of the foliage in the fall.

P. laurocerasus Cherry laurel,

English laurel
E. Europe, Asia Minor.
FULLY HARDY.
Large oblong leaves, dark green and glossy, on a vigorous shade-tolerant shrub that often grows to 20ft (6m) make this popular as an evergreen screening plant. It is often cut back annually to make an informal hedge, as it can have a spread to 25ft (7.5m) or more, and grown in this way the plant retains its racemes of white flowers, which are followed by cherry-like fruits. Hedges of erect and bushy cultivars such as **'Rotundifolia'** can be given a more formal outline but the trimming should be done with secateurs so that whole leaves or sprays of leaves are removed. Plants can also be trained to make dome-headed standards. The cherry laurel does not do well on thin chalky soils but otherwise tolerates a wide range of conditions.
P. lusitanica Portugal cherry laurel
S.W. Europe.
FULLY HARDY.
The Portugal laurel is more refined than the cherry laurel and is also hardier and tolerant of lime. The red of the stalks contrasts with the dark green of the pointed glossy leaves. On untrimmed plants racemes of white flowers are borne in summer and followed by red to deep purple fruit. It is grown as an informal screening hedge but is also trimmed more formally, easily making a hedge to a height of 13ft (4m). **'Myrtifolia,'** which is relatively slow-growing and has small leaves, is particularly suitable for training as a dome-headed standard.
P. spinosa Blackthorn, sloe
Europe and N. Africa to W. Asia.
FULLY HARDY.
The blackthorn, the source of sloes for flavoring gin, is a deciduous thorny small tree that grows to about 15ft (4.5m). In parts of Europe it is a conspicuous constituent of hedgerows in early spring, when the branches are covered in masses of snowy flowers. Its thorniness makes it particularly useful in a laid hedge forming a stock barrier on farmland. The blackthorn is also attractive in an ornamental rustic hedge but its suckering habit counts against it in more ordered parts of the garden.

PLANTING/SPACING
Deciduous between mid-fall and late winter, evergreens in mid- to late spring.
P. x *cistena* and *P. spinosa* 12–18in (30–45cm), other deciduous *Prunus* 18–24in (45–60cm) and evergreens 24–36in (60–90cm).
MAINTENANCE Trim once or twice annually in summer, when there is least likelihood of silver leaf infection.
PROPAGATION Deciduous species named here from greenwood cuttings in early summer or, as evergreens, from semi-ripe cuttings in mid-summer.
PROBLEMS Aphids, borers, caterpillars; canker, leaf spot (*P. laurocerasus*), scale.

QUERCUS OAK
The oaks, a large northern hemisphere genus of about 400 species, include deciduous, semi-evergreen and evergreen trees and shrubs, some of which tolerate shaping. In traditional woodland management two European species, *Q. petraea*, the durmast oak, and *Q. robur*, the English oak, were frequently pollarded, regular cutting back ensuring a supply of timber.
Q. ilex Holm oak
S.W. Europe. FROST HARDY.
The least ordered part of the Italian garden is the *bosco*, the shady grove planted with evergreen oaks. These same oaks are often used in many parts of the world as windbreaks in coastal areas and can be trimmed to form tall hedges, or massive but simple topiary shapes, such as drums and mopheads. The somber green of the oaks makes this large-scale topiary impressively solemn.

PLANTING Early fall or mid- to late spring. Hedge spacing 24in (60cm).
MAINTENANCE Trim annually in late summer.
PROPAGATION From seed, in fall.
PROBLEMS Aphids, gall wasps; fungal diseases, including bracket fungi.

RHAMNUS
There are over 100 species of deciduous and evergreen shrubs and trees, many of them thorny, and some on that account make useful hedges. One of these is *R. cathartica*, the

common buckthorn, a widely distributed deciduous species that does best on moist soils.
R. alaternus Italian buckthorn
Mediterranean, Ukraine.
FROST HARDY.
This evergreen shrub, with glossy dark green leaves, was much used in the 17th century for hedges and topiary. Its lack of hardiness counts against it, but where the climate is mild enough it can make hedges up to about 8ft (2.5m) high in sunny well-drained conditions. The gray tones and cream margin of **'Argenteovariegata'** make it a particularly attractive variegated plant for simple topiary shapes, such as balls on clear stems. It is, however, less hardy than the plain-leaved Italian buckthorn.

PLANTING/SPACING In mid- to late spring. 18–24in (45–60cm).
MAINTENANCE Trim two or three times annually, between early summer and early fall.
PROPAGATION From semi-ripe cuttings in summer.
PROBLEMS Usually none.

ROSMARINUS ROSEMARY
There are two species and one has long been valued as a medicinal and culinary herb and has been much used in the past to make aromatic hedges.
R. officinalis Rosemary
Mediterranean. FROST HARDY.
The herb of remembrance is an evergreen shrub that is densely covered with gray-green needle-like leaves, paler and felted on the underside, which readily release their invigorating fragrance when touched. Blue flowers, usually pale but there are dark- and white-flowered forms, appear in spring. Rosemary is a sun-loving plant and needs free-draining soil, but this does not need to be rich and lime is not a problem. In cold gardens it needs a warm sheltered position. Some rosemaries are spreading, even sprawling, but it is the more typically upright cultivars 40–60in (1–1.5m) in height that are suited to planting as hedges. One of the most erect and vigorous rosemaries is **'Miss Jessopp's Upright,'** which is suitable for a hedge to a height of about 4ft (1.2m). In the

past rosemary has been used for topiary. The best results are achieved by training a simple ball on a clear stem about 24in (60cm) high.

PLANTING/SPACING In early to mid-spring. 18–24in (45–60cm).
MAINTENANCE Clip twice annually, in early summer after flowering and again in late summer.
PROPAGATION From semi-ripe cuttings in summer or from hard-wood cuttings taken in early fall.
PROBLEMS Usually none.

SANTOLINA
The 18 species are aromatic evergreen shrubs of dry rocky slopes in the Mediterranean. Several are widely used as front-of-border plants in sunny well-drained conditions but for shaping into low hedges the best is undoubtedly cotton lavender.
S. chamaecyparissus Cotton lavender
S. France. FROST HARDY.
The silver-gray mound of finely dissected leaves, up to 24in (60cm) high, is topped in summer by lemon-yellow button flowers, although these are lost if plants are trimmed several times in summer. Low hedges in knot gardens or edging beds can be trimmed to a height of about 18in (45cm).

PLANTING/SPACING In spring. 12in (30cm).
MAINTENANCE Clip in spring and then two or three times in the summer or, for a looser effect, in spring and then immediately after flowering.
PROPAGATION From semi-ripe cuttings in mid- to late summer.
PROBLEMS Usually none.

TAXUS YEW
The yews, a small genus of evergreen conifers, include topiary and hedging plants of superlative quality. They grow more slowly than most other conifers suitable for hedging but even so make steady growth, responding to clipping by developing dense, fine-textured surfaces that will retain sharp angles and details. Major failures are often the result of the plants being set too deep or of inadequate drainage. The toxicity of all parts of the plant other than the aril (the fleshy surround

to the seed) makes yews unsuitable for planting next to land where animals graze.

T. baccata Common yew, English yew
Europe and N. Africa to Iran.
FULLY HARDY.
Good drainage is essential but the yew's tolerance of a wide range of growing conditions, including exposure, shade and soils that range from acidic to strongly alkaline, make it a very adaptable hedging and topiary plant. The type is ideal for hedges up to 20ft (6m) high, its dense growth making dark green architecture that has a somber beauty of its own and is a perfect foil for brighter, more colorful plants. Clean-lined or rounded large-scale topiary can be shaped from a single plant or several trimmed as one. The best of the golden yews, which are generally less vigorous than the type, is **T.b. 'Elegantissima.'**
T.b. 'Fastigiata,' the Irish yew, which forms a narrow column when young, is difficult to maintain as a simple vertical accent. One solution is to restrict growth to four or five stems forming a cluster of uprights. Binding in the branches with hoops of wire, the traditional technique to keep plants columnar, causes problems of its own but, once started, is difficult to abandon.
T. × media Anglojap yew
FULLY HARDY.
This hybrid, raised in Massachusetts, U.S.A., shows the vigor of one parent, **T. baccata**, and the hardiness of its other parent, the more shrubby **T. cuspidata**, the Japanese yew. Cultivars that make excellent dark green hedges include the slow-growing **T. × m. 'Brownii,'** suitable for hedges up to 8ft (2.5m) high, and the more vigorous and erect **T. × m. 'Hicksii.'**

PLANTING/SPACING Between mid-fall and mid-spring. 18–24in (45–60cm).
MAINTENANCE Clip once annually, in mid- to late summer, or, ideally, in early to mid-summer followed by a light trim in early fall. Renovate topiary and hedges in early spring.
PROPAGATION From semi-ripe cuttings of upright shoots in late summer or early fall; from seed sown in the fall.

PROBLEMS Mealy bug, black vine weevil, yew scale; *Phytophthora* root rot.

THUJA ARBORVITAE
Of the half-dozen species of these evergreen conifers two are particularly useful hedging plants. The aromatic foliage consists of scale-like leaves forming fanned sprays. Both species are best suited to soils that are moist but well drained and positions in full sun that are sheltered from cold winds. The white cedar is the hardier of the two. Young plants of the western red cedar need screening from prevailing winds until they are established.
T. occidentalis White cedar
E. North America. FULLY HARDY.
This slow-growing columnar tree is suitable for hedges up to about 13ft (4m) high. It has dull green leaves, paler on the underside, and the foliage often takes on a bronze tint in winter. There are numerous dwarf cultivars of naturally tight shapes.
T. plicata Western red cedar
W. North America. FULLY HARDY.
This fast-growing species, which has drooping sprays of glossy rich green foliage, is suitable for hedges up to about 16ft (5m) high. **'Atrovirens'** is a very deep green. The variegation of **'Zebrina,'** suitable for hedges up to about 11½ft (3.5m), creates a gold effect.

PLANTING/SPACING In early fall or mid- to late spring. 24in (60cm).
MAINTENANCE Clip twice annually, in late spring and late summer.
PROPAGATION From semi-ripe cuttings in late summer.
PROBLEMS Aphids, bag worm, mealy bugs, scale insects; canker, die-back of *T. plicata* caused by a fungal disease (*Keithia*), leaf blight.

TILIA LINDEN
The lindens are deciduous trees of the temperate northern hemisphere, many with attractive fluttering foliage and numerous small flowers that exhale one of the most intoxicating fragrances of summer. Lindens have been much used as avenue trees but their flexible growth makes them particularly suitable for pleaching. In the past **T. × europaea**, the common linden,

was very widely planted, but two disadvantages—its tendency to sucker and its proneness to aphid attack—mean that other lindens less troubled by these problems are now generally planted in its place.
T. × euchlora FULLY HARDY.
The dark glossy leaves show their pale undersides when caught by a breeze. This linden has often been planted as an alternative to *T. × europaea* because it does not produce suckers and resists aphid attack. However, the flowers are narcotic to bees, which in their dazed state may present a hazard, particularly to children. This linden is vulnerable to bacterial slime flux disease.
T. platyphyllos Large-leaved linden
Europe. FULLY HARDY.
This linden is coarser than *T. × euchlora*, and left to itself makes a large tree with heart-shaped leaves that are pale to mid-green and downy on the underside. Aphids are a problem and it suckers, but not as freely as *T. × europaea*. The favored form of it for pleaching is **'Rubra,'** the red-twigged linden, with pliable stems that have red shoots in winter.

PLANTING/SPACING Between fall and late winter. 6½–13ft (2–4m).
MAINTENANCE Prune in fall but train in growth as required in summer.
PROPAGATION From suckers in fall; by layering in spring or summer.
PROBLEMS Aphids (sooty mold develops on the secreted honeydew), caterpillars, linden mite, scale insects; anthracnose, *Phytophthora* root rot.

TSUGA HEMLOCK
The hemlocks, of which there are about ten species in all, are evergreen conifers that as specimens develop into elegant cone-shaped trees.
T. canadensis, the eastern hemlock, which is very hardy and tolerant of lime, can be used as a hedging plant but is surpassed in quality by the western hemlock.
T. heterophylla Western hemlock
W. North America. FULLY HARDY.
The fast-growing western hemlock, in the wild distributed from Alaska to California, has flattened needle-like leaves that are dark green on the upper surface and paler on the underside. It

does best on neutral to acid soils and needs a plentiful supply of moisture in a sheltered position. Its tolerance of shade is a considerable advantage.

PLANTING/SPACING In mid-fall or early to mid-spring. 24in (60cm).
MAINTENANCE In the case of this conifer it is advisable to pinch out the growing tip to encourage bushy growth. Trim twice annually between early summer and early fall.
PROPAGATION From seed in spring; from semi-ripe cuttings in late summer or early fall.
PROBLEMS Bag worm, scale insect; rust, sensitive to environmental pollution.

VIBURNUM
The genus comprises about 150 species of deciduous and evergreen shrubs and small trees. Laurustinus was often grown as a clipped plant in the late 16th and 17th centuries.
V. tinus Laurustinus
Mediterranean. FULLY HARDY.
When not trimmed laurustinus can easily grow to 10ft (3m) or more in height and spread, and is densely clothed with dark green leaves on reddish shoots. In damp weather the plant gives off an unpleasant smell. If plants are trimmed only lightly in early summer the winter display of white flowers, which are pink in bud, is not greatly reduced. The cultivars with comparatively small leaves, such as **'Eve Price'** and **'Gwenllian,'** are those best suited for more formal shaping as hedges or simple topiary such as balls or domes on clear stems.
PLANTING/SPACING In early to mid-fall or mid- to late spring. 18–24in (45–60cm).
MAINTENANCE Clip twice annually, in early and late summer.
PROPAGATION From semi-ripe cuttings in summer; from seed sown in fall.
PROBLEMS Aphids, scale insect, whitefly; leaf spot.

PLANTS FOR SPECIAL PURPOSES

STANDARDS
Ornamental shrubs to grow as flowering or fruiting standards
Brugmansia × *candida* (angels' trumpets) min. 45°F (7°C)
Argyranthemum frutescens HALF-HARDY
Chamelaucium uncinatum HALF-HARDY
× *Citrofortunella microcarpa* (calamondin) HALF-HARDY
Colutea arborescens (bladder senna) FULLY HARDY
Fortunella japonica (round kumquat) min. 45°F (7°C)
Fuchsia hybrids HALF-HARDY TO FROST HARDY
Gardenia augusta (common gardenia) min. 50°F (10°C)
Heliotropium arborescens (Heliotrope) HALF-HARDY
Hibiscus rosa-sinensis (Chinese hibiscus) min. 50°F (10°C)
Hydrangea macrophylla (common hydrangea) FULLY HARDY
Lagerstroemia indica (crepe flower, crepe myrtle) HALF-HARDY TO FROST HARDY
Lantana camara FROST TENDER min. 50°F (10°C)
Leptospermum scoparium HALF-HARDY
Nerium oleander (rose bay) min. 36°F (2°C)
Pelargonium hybrids min. 36°F (2°C)
Rosa hybrids (Rose) FULLY HARDY
Salix caprea 'Kilmarnock' (Kilmarnock willow) FULLY HARDY
Solanum rantonnetii (Blue potato bush) min. 45°F (7°C)
Tibouchina urvilleana (Brazilian spider flower) min. 39°F (3°C)
Viburnum tinus (laurustinus) FULLY HARDY

Climbers to train as standards
Ampelopsis glandulosa var. *brevipedunculata* 'Elegans' FROST HARDY TO FULLY HARDY
Bougainvillea × *buttiana* HALF-HARDY
Lonicera periclymenum (common honeysuckle) FULLY HARDY
Vitis vinifera (grapevine) FULLY HARDY
Wisteria sinensis FULLY HARDY

TRAINED IVY
Small-leaved ivies to train on frames
All of the following are frost hardy to fully hardy trailing cultivars of the common ivy (*Hedera helix*) with leaves ¾–1½in (2–4cm) long.
Plain-leaved
'Asterisk,' 'Cascade,' 'Duckfoot,' 'Midget,' 'Pin Oak,' 'Triton'
Variegated (cream or yellow)
'Ambrosia,' 'Chester,' 'Eva,' 'Goldchild'
Variegated (white or grey)
'Glacier,' 'Little Diamond'

HEDGES
Most of the plants in the following selections are best trimmed only lightly, although some tolerate more rigorous shaping.

Deciduous and semi-evergreen shrubs and trees for informal hedges

To 6½ft (2m) or more
Acer campestre FULLY HARDY
Cotoneaster franchetii FULLY HARDY
C. simonsii FULLY HARDY
Corylus avellana FULLY HARDY
C. maxima 'Purpurea' FULLY HARDY
Euonymus alatus (winged spindle) FULLY HARDY
Fuchsia magellanica FROST HARDY
Lagerstroemia indica (crepe myrtle) FROST HARDY
Poncirus trifoliata (Japanese bitter orange) FULLY HARDY
Ribes sanguineum (flowering currant) FULLY HARDY
Rosa xanthia 'Canary Bird' FULLY HARDY
Tamarix ramosissima (tamarisk) FULLY HARDY
T. tetandra (tamarisk) FULLY HARDY

2–5ft (60–150cm)
Abelia 'Edward Goucher' FROST HARDY
Berberis thunbergii f. *atropurpurea* FULLY HARDY
Chaenomeles speciosa FULLY HARDY
Forsythia × *intermedia* FULLY HARDY
Potentilla fruticosa 'Vilmoriniana' FULLY HARDY
Rosa 'Blanche Double de Coubert' FULLY HARDY
R. 'Pink Grootendorst' FULLY HARDY
Symphoricarpos × *doorenbosii* (snowberry) FULLY HARDY

Under 24in (60cm)
Berberis thunbergii 'Bagatelle' FULLY HARDY

Evergreen shrubs and trees for informal hedges

To 6½ft (2m) or more
Acca sellowiana (pineapple guava) FROST HARDY
Aucuba japonica 'Crotonifolia' (spotted laurel) FULLY HARDY
Azara microphylla FULLY HARDY
Berberis darwinii FULLY HARDY
B. julianae FULLY HARDY
B. × *stenophylla* FULLY HARDY
Callistemon citrinus 'Splendens' HALF-HARDY
Camellia sasanqua FROST HARDY TO FULLY HARDY
Cephalotaxus harringtonia FULLY HARDY
Cassinia leptophylla subsp. *fulvida* (golden heather) FROST HARDY TO FULLY HARDY
Coprosma repens (looking-glass plant) HALF-HARDY
Corokia cotoneaster (wire-netting bush) FROST HARDY
Cotoneaster lacteus FULLY HARDY
C. salicifolius FULLY HARDY
Dodonaea viscosa 'Purpurea' HALF-HARDY
Elaeagnus × *ebbingei* and cvs FULLY HARDY
E. pungens and cvs FULLY HARDY
Escallonia hybrids FROST HARDY TO FULLY HARDY
E. rubra 'Crimson Spire' FULLY HARDY
Eugenia myrtifolia HALF-HARDY
Euonymus japonicus (Japanese spindle) FROST HARDY
Grevillea rosmarinifolia FROST HARDY
Griselinia littoralis (broadleaf) FROST HARDY TO FULLY HARDY
Leptospermum scoparium (manuka, New Zealand tea tree) HALF-HARDY TO FROST HARDY
Myoporum laetum (ngaio) min. 36°F (2°C)
Nerium oleander (rose bay) min. 36°F (2°C)
Olearia macrodonta (arorangi) FROST HARDY TO FULLY HARDY
O. traversii FROST HARDY TO FULLY HARDY
Osmanthus delavayi FROST HARDY
O. heterophyllus FULLY HARDY
Photinia × *fraseri* FROST HARDY
Podocarpus totara (totara) FROST HARDY
Pyracantha hybrids (firethorn) FROST HARDY TO FULLY HARDY

20–60in (60–150m)
Berberis gagnepainii var. *lanceifolia* FULLY HARDY
Choisya ternata (Mexican orange blossom) FULLY HARDY
Cotoneaster integrifolius FULLY HARDY

Euonymus fortunei 'Emerald Gaiety' FULLY HARDY
Olearia × *haastii* FULLY HARDY
Osmanthus × *burkwoodii* FULLY HARDY
Podocarpus nivalis (alpine totara) FULLY HARDY
Prostanthera cuneata (alpine mint bush) FROST HARDY
Rhaphiolepis umbellata FROST HARDY
Sarcococca confusa FULLY HARDY
Teucrium fruticans (shrubby germander, tree germander) FROST HARDY
Ugni molinae (Chilean guava) HALF-HARDY
Westringia fruticosa (Australian rosemary) min. 41°F (5°C)

Under 24in (60cm)
Berberis buxifolia 'Pygmaea' FULLY HARDY

FRUIT
Fruit trees or fruit bushes for restricted shapes
For compact standards
apple (on dwarfing rootstock), fig, gooseberry, peach (genetic dwarf), red currant
For espaliers
apple, pear
For cordons
apple, gooseberry, pear
For fans
apple, apricot, cherry (acid, duke and sweet), currant (red and white), fig, nectarine, peach, pear

CLIMBERS
Vigorous climbers for arbors
The following is a selection of vigorous climbers that can be trained on arbors to create shade.

Actinidia deliciosa (Chinese gooseberry, kiwi fruit) FROST HARDY
Ampelopsis brevipedunculata FULLY HARDY
Campsis × *tagliabuana* 'Madame Galen' FROST HARDY
Clematis armandii FROST HARDY
C. montana FULLY HARDY
Eccremocarpus scaber (Chilean glory vine) FROST HARDY
Hedera colchica 'Dentata Variegata' FULLY HARDY
Jasminum officinale (common jasmine) FROST HARDY
Lonicera × *brownii* 'Dropmore Scarlet' FULLY HARDY
Pandorea jasminoides min. 41°F (5°C)
P. pandorana (bower plant) min. 41°F (5°C)

Podranea ricasoliana (pink trumpet vine) min. 50°F (10°C)
Solandra maxima (cup of gold) min. 50°F (10°C)
Thunbergia grandiflora (Bengal clock vine, blue trumpet vine) min. 50°F (10°C)
Vitis 'Brant' FULLY HARDY
V. coignetiae FULLY HARDY
V. vinifera 'Purpurea' FULLY HARDY
Wisteria floribunda FULLY HARDY
W. sinensis FULLY HARDY

Roses suitable for training on ropes
The following vigorous climbing and rambling roses, all fully hardy, have stems that are pliant enough to train closely to supports such as ropes hanging in curves between pillars.
Rosa 'Adélaïde d'Orléans'
R. 'Albéric Barbier'
R. 'Evangeline'
R. 'François Juranville'
R. 'Madame Alfred Carrière'
R. 'Madame Grégoire Staechelin'
R. 'Debutante'
R. 'Rambling Rector'
R. 'Seagull'
R. 'Silver Moon'

KNOT GARDENS
Traditional plants for knot gardens
The following plants, mainly aromatic and all of them fully hardy, were much used in English knot gardens in the 16th and 17th centuries.
bee balm *see* lemon balm
camomile *Chamaemelum nobile*
carnations derived from *Dianthus caryophyllus*
cotton lavender *Santolina chamaecyparissus*
germander *Teucrium* × *lucidrys*
hyssop *Hyssopus officinalis*
lavender *Lavandula angustifolia*
lemon balm *Melissa officinalis*
marjoram, common *Origanum vulgare*
pinks derived from *Dianthus plumarius*
rosemary *Rosmarinus officinalis*
rue *Ruta graveolens*
sage *Salvia officinalis*
southernwood *Artemisia abrotanum*
thrift *Armeria maritima*
thyme, common *Thymus vulgaris*
thyme, wild *Thymus serpyllum*
winter savory *Satureja montana*

Plant hardiness zones of North America

Plants that are successful in your zone and in zones with numbers lower than yours should survive winters in your garden.

Average minimum winter temperatures

Zone 1 below -50°F/below -45°C

Zone 2 -50° to -40°F/-45° to -40°C

Zone 3 -40° to -30°F/-40° to -35°C

Zone 4 -30° to -20°F/-35° to -29°C

Zone 5 -20° to -10°F/-29° to -23°C

Zone 6 -10° to 0°F/-23° to -18°C

Zone 7 0° to 10°F/-18° to -12°C

Zone 8 10° to 20°F/-12° to -6°C

Zone 9 20° to 30°F/-6° to -1°C

Zone 10 30° to 40°F/-1° to 4.5°C

Gardens to visit

Due to space limitations, it was not possible to include the author's recommendations on topiary gardens in Europe and North America that are open for public viewing. However, if you wish to receive a list of David Joyce's recommended topiary gardens, please send a business-sized SASE, in the U.S. to: Topiary Gardens, Firefly Books (U.S.) Inc., P.O. Box 1338, Ellicott Station, Buffalo, New York, 14205; and in Canada to: Topiary Gardens, Firefly Books Ltd., 3680 Victoria Park Avenue, Willowdale, Ontario, M2H 3K1. Allow 4-6 weeks for receipt.

Sources

SEEDLINGS
Barber Nursery
14282 Rogers Road
Willis, Texas 77378
Tel (409) 856-8074
Caroline jasmine, American holly, crape myrtle, sweetgum, oaks, vines and plants that thrive in the south. Free price list. Canada and US.

Bay Laurel Nursery
2500 El Camino Real
Atascadero, California 93422
Tel (805) 466-3406
Fax (805) 466-6455
Fruit trees, ornamental trees and shrubs. U.S. only.

Bear Creek Nursery
PO Box 411
Northport, Washington 99157
Tel (509) 732-6219
Fax (509) 732-4417
Cold- and drought-hardy northern-grown stocks. 284 antique and new apple varieties, plus Asian Pear, cherry, nectarine and more. Also English oak and European beech. U.S. only.

Camellia Forest Nursery
125 Carolina Forest
Chapel Hill, North Carolina 27516
Tel (919) 968-0504 or 967-5529
Fax (919) 967-5529
www.camforest.com
Cold-hardy camellias, trees and

shrubs from China and Japan. Dwarf chamaecyparis, junipers, thuja, tsuga. Catalog $2.

Corn Hill Nursery, Ltd.
RR 5, Route 890
Petitcodiac, New Brunswick
Canada E0A 2H0
Tel (506) 756-3635
Fax (506) 756-1087
Known for roses, they also supply flowering shrubs, fruit trees and vines.

Fairweather Gardens
PO Box 330
Greenwich, New Jersey 08323
Tel (609) 451-6261
Fax (609) 451-0303
Viburnums plus ornamental trees and shrubs, including camellias, hollies, magnolias, oaks. Catalog $3. U.S. only.

Forestfarm
990 Tetherow Road
Williams, Oregon 97544
Tel (541) 846-7269
Fax (541) 846-6963
www.forestfarm.com
Wide selection of shade trees, vines and ground covers, hedge plants, conifers, ornamentals. Catalog $4. U.S. and Canada.

Heronswood Nursery
7530 NE 228th Street
Kingston, Washington 98346
Tel (360) 297-4172
Fax (360) 297-8321
www.heronswood.com
Rare trees, shrubs, vines, conifers, tender perennials, grasses. Catalog $8.

Holly Ridge Nursery
5925 South Ridge Road West
Geneva, Ohio 44041
Toll-Free 1-800-465-5901
Tel (440) 466-0134
Fax (440) 466-1272
www.hollyridgenursery.com
Ilex meservae, verticillata and over 40 varieties of *Ilex opaca*, plus azalea, buxus, lilac and viburnum. All hardy zones 4–6.

Hortico Nurseries Inc.
723 Robson Road, RR 1
Waterdown, Ontario
Canada L0R 2H1
Tel (905) 689-6984
24-Hour Fax (905) 689-6566
Individual shrub catalog. $3.

Musser Forests, Inc.
PO Box 340 Rt. 119 North
Indiana, Pennsylvania 15701
Toll-Free 1-800-643-8319 (U.S. only)
Tel (724) 465-5685
Fax (724) 465-9893
Northern grown evergreen and hard-wood seedlings, plus groundcovers, juniper, yew, arborvitae, hemlock.

Oikos Tree Crops
PO Box 19425
Kalamazoo, Michigan 49019-0425
Tel (616) 624-6233
Fax (616) 342-2759
Species and hybrid oaks, plus nut trees, American native edibles, deciduous magnolias and other unusual ornamental trees and shrubs. U.S. and Canada.

Raintree Nursery
391 Butts Road
Morton, Washington 98356
Tel (360) 496-6400
Toll-Free Fax 1-888-770-8358
Fax (360) 496-6465
www.raintreenursery.com
Hardy, resistant fruit and nut trees, vines. Free 80-page guidebook/catalog. U.S. only.

Sonoma Antique Apple Nursery
4395 Westside Road
Healdsburg, California 95448
Tel (707) 433 6420
www.applenursery.com
All variety of organically grown fruit trees, including apple, apricot, cherry, fig, nut, peaches, pears and plums and more. Ships to U.S. only.

Stark Brothers
PO Box 10
Louisiana, Missouri 63353-0010
Toll-Free 1-800-325-4180
www.starkbros.com
Almost exclusively fruit trees, and a few ornamentals. U.S. only.

Topiary Gardens
1840 Stump Road
Marcellus, New York 13108
Tel/Fax (315) 673-9016
Hard-to-find ornamental shrubs, trees. 300 varieties of Japanese maple plus unique conifers. Tools. Catalog $2. U.S. only (not WA, CA, HI, PR, AK).

Wavecrest Nursery
2509 Lakeshore Drive
Fennville, Michigan 49408

Tel (616) 543-4175
Fax (616) 543-4100
Boxwood, hornbeam, hawthorn, beech, holly, cedar, yew, hedges, fruit trees.

Wayside Gardens
1 Garden Lane
Hodges, SC 29695-0001
Tel (800) 845 1124
Fax (800) 817 1124
www.waysidegardens.com
Wide range of trees, shrubs and perennials. Free catalog (U.S. only)

TOOLS

De Van Koek
3600 Silver Dollar Circle
Austin, Texas 78744
Tel (512) 339-0009
Fax (512) 386-6401
Importer and seller of superb European tools.

Forestry Suppliers, Inc.
PO Box 8397
205 West Rankin Street
Jackson, Mississippi 39284-8397
Toll-Free 1-800-647-5368 (U.S.)
Tel (601) 354-3565
Toll-Free Fax 1-800-543-4203
www.forestry-suppliers.com
High-quality tools used by outdoor professionals, including many fine, unusual tools for arboriculture and the home gardener.

Kinsman Company Inc.
PO Box 357
River Road
Point Pleasant
Pennsylvania 18950-0357
Toll-Free 1-800-733-4146
Fax (215) 297-0450
www.kinsman.garden com.
Wide range of tools and accessories.

Langenbach
644 Enterprise Avenue
Galesburg, Illinois 61401
Toll-Free 1-800-362-1991
www.langenbach.com
Fine tools from around the world.

A.M. Leonard, Inc.
PO Box 816
241 Fox Drive
Piqua, Ohio 45356
Toll-Free 1-800-543-8955
Toll-Free Fax 1-800-433-0633
www.amleo.com
Wide range of tools used by professionals.

TOPIARY FRAMES, GARDEN POTS

EadyTown Topiary Nursery
113 Belle Oaks Lane
Pineville, South Carolina 29468-3429
Tel (843) 351-4558
Fax (843) 351-4958
www.eadytown.com
Large selection of animal topiary wire frames from small to large garden size. Also custom designs and builds to specifications. U.S. and Canada.

Seibert & Rice
PO Box 365
Short Hills, New Jersey 07078
Tel (973) 467-8266
www.seibert-rice.com
Fine terra cotta pottery handmade in Impruneta, Italy, including classic lion's head and rolled rim designs. Can be left outdoors year round in very cold climates. Catalog $5.

Topiary Art Works & Greenhouses
PO Box 574
9926 S 151 West
Clearwater, Kansas 67026
Toll-Free 1-800-355-3110
Tel (316) 584-2366
Fax (316) 584-2227
www.topiaryartworks.com
Fanciful life and over-life size topiary frames, stuffed with sphagnum moss or finished-planted. Standard drawings and models or custom-made. U.S. and Canada.

TopiaryInc
4520 Watrous Avenue
Tampa, Florida 33629
Tel (813) 286-8626 or (813) 839-1547
Fax (813) 282-9345
www.topiaryinc.com
Hand-crafted wire forms, welded from galvanized steel wire, and painted. U.S. and Canada.

P. Wakefield & Co., Ltd.
139 E. Rockdale Road
Cambridge, Wisconsin 53523
Tel (608) 423-7060
Fax (608) 423-7184
www.pwakefield.com
Traditional garden pottery in the manner of 18th- & 19th-century English, French & Tuscan potters. Terra-cotta moss finish, traditional English painted "work pots" and iron garden accessories.

Index

Numbers in *italic* refer to illustration captions. Common names for plants are cross-referenced to botanical names. See also listings of plants in the Directory, pages 148–54.

Acknowledgments

AUTHOR'S ACKNOWLEDGMENTS
It is a pleasure to acknowledge my debt to many gardeners for the inspiration of their garden craft, and to them and past and present writers on gardening for information on the shaping and training of plants. Many people have played a role in the making of this book. I am particularly grateful to Anne Askwith and Sara Robin, who have been closely involved in editorial and design matters, to Laura Stoddart, who has added so much to the book's appeal with her beautiful illustrations of the garden plans, and to Clare Roberts, who has executed clear instructional artwork. I would also like to thank Helen Baz, Serena Dilnot, John Elsley and Tony Lord. I owe much to the helpfulness of the following members of the editorial, design and picture research teams at Frances Lincoln: Thomas Armstrong, Jo Christian, Anne Fraser, Sue Gladstone, Trish Going, Caroline Hillier, Louise Kirby, Sarah Mitchell and Tom Windross. In mentioning them by name I am conscious that many other members of staff are deserving of thanks even when I am ignorant of the part they have played in the production and promotion of this book.

HORTICULTURAL CONSULTANT
Tony Lord
PROJECT EDITOR Jo Christian
EDITOR Anne Askwith
STEP BY STEP ARTWORK Clare Roberts
INDEX Helen Baz
ART EDITORS Louise Kirby, Sara Robin
PICTURE RESEARCH Sue Gladstone
PRODUCTION Stephan Stuart

EDITORIAL DIRECTOR Kate Cave
ART DIRECTOR Caroline Hillier
HEAD OF PICTURES Anne Fraser

PHOTOGRAPHIC ACKNOWLEDGMENTS
A=above   B=below   L=left
C=centre   R=right

Nicola Browne 45 (designer W. & F. Van Glabbeek), 58 (Prionia-tuinen; designer Henk Gerritsen), 60AR (designer W. & F. Van Glabbeek), 65 (designer W. & F. Van Glabbeek) Garden Picture Library/Marijke Heuff 33, John Glover 101, Brigitte Thomas 146

John Glover 55, 98

Jerry Harpur 4R & 90 (designer Lon Shapiro, San Francisco), 5B & 87 (Manor House, Bledlow, Bucks), 10 (Château Gourdon, Grasse, France), 21 (Nicholas Haslam, King Henry's Hunting Lodge), 25R (La Casella, Le Rouret, France), 26 (Saling Hall, Great Saling, Essex), 48–49 (Manor House, Bledlow, Bucks), 53 (Ladew Gardens, Maryland), 68 (Hatfield House, Hertfordshire), 70 (Château de Corbeil-Cerf, France; designer René Pechère), 71 (Bourton House, Gloucestershire), 81 (Château de Corbeil-Cerf; designer René Pechère), 83A (Château de Corbeil-Cerf; designer René Pechère), 87 (Manor House, Bledlow, Bucks), 112R (Helmingham Hall, Suffolk), 115 (Nooroo, Mt. Wilson, New South Wales, designer Peter Valder), 140 (Bourton House, Gloucestershire)

Marcus Harpur 4L & 20 (designer Jonathan Baillie, London), 88 (The Gibberd Garden, Harlow, Essex)

Marijke Heuff 5CR & 60B (Mr & Mrs Dekker, Veere, Holland), 7 (De Hagenhof, Angeren, Holland), 8 (designer Marc De Winter; Halle-Zoersel, Belgium), 9 (De Heerenhof, Maastricht, Holland), 12 (Ineke Greve, Heerlen, Holland), 29 (Mr & Mrs Dekker, Veere, Holland), 39 (Hodges Barn, Shipton Moyne, Gloucestershire), 60AL (Walda Pairon, Heide, Belgium), 61A (designer Marc De Winter; Halle Zoersel, Belgium), 73 (Miep Maarse, Aalsmeer, Holland), 80 (De Heerenhof, Maastricht, Holland), 93 (Nijsingh Huis, Eelde, Holland), 94 (Ineke Greve, Heerlen, Holland), 95 (designer Marc De Winter; Halle-Zoersel, Belgium), 103 (De Heerenhof, Maastricht, Holland), 106 (Mr and Mrs Van Heuven, Markeld, Holland), 107 (Ineke Greve, Heerlen, Holland), 116 (Ineke Greve, Heerlen, Holland), 126 (designer Marc De Winter; Halle-Zoersel, Belgium)

Saxon Holt 144A

Andrea Jones 145 (Villandry, France)

Michèle Lamontagne 6 (Levens Hall, Cumbria), 15, 66

Andrew Lawson 2 (Westwell Manor, Oxfordshire; designer Anthea Gibson), 5A & 130 (private garden, Worcestershire), 5CL (Wilton House, Wiltshire), 22 (Rofford Manor, Oxfordshire), 25L (Japanese Artists Garden, Chelsea 1996), 30 (The Hempel, London; designer Anouska Hempel), 31L (designer Mirabel Osler), 31R (Badminton House, Gloucestershire), 34 (Westwell Manor, Oxfordshire; designer Anthea Gibson), 35 (Alderley Grange, Gloucestershire), 36 (Wilton House, Wiltshire), 37 (Knightshayes Court, Devon), 42, 46, 51 (designer Rani Lall, Oxford), 52, 56 (private garden, Lancashire; designer Arabella Lennox-Boyd), 61B (Court Farm, Broadway, Worcestershire), 62, 63 (Madingly Hall, Cambridge), 77 (Levens Hall, Cumbria), 78–9 (Stobshiels House, East Lothian, Scotland), 82 (Westwell Manor, Oxfordshire; designer Anthea Gibson), 83B (Gothic House, Oxfordshire), 84 (Badminton House, Gloucestershire), 97 (Nymans Gardens, West Sussex), 99A (West Green, Hampshire; designer Marylyn Abbott), 99B (Vann, Surrey), 102 (The Grove, Oxfordshire; designer the late David Hicks), 111 (House of Pitmuies, Forfar, Scotland), 112L (Daylesford Garden), 113 (Gothic House, Oxfordshire), 117 (The Old Rectory, Sudborough, Northamptonshire), 119, 120, 121 (The Old Rectory, Sudborough, Northamptonshire), 125 (Powis Castle, Powys, Wales), 131 (Abbotswood, Gloucestershire), 135A (private garden, Barnsley, Gloucestershire; designer Rosemary Verey), 135B (The Laskett, Herefordshire; designers Roy Strong & Julia Trevelyan Oman), 136 (Pitmedden Garden, Grampian, Scotland), 137 (Wilton House, Wiltshire; designer Xa Tollemache), 138 (Pitmedden Garden, Grampian, Scotland), 142 (Westwell Manor, Oxfordshire; designer Anthea Gibson), 143 (Château Villandry, France), 144B (Kennerton Green, Mittagong, New South Wales; designer Marylyn Abbott)

Tony Lord 89 (Packwood House, Warwickshire)

Clive Nichols Garden Pictures 74 (Chenies Manor, Buckinghamshire)

Hugh Palmer 11 (Herren Hausen, Hanover)

Erika R. Shank 17

Derek St Romaine 41, 64, 128–129 (Helmingham Hall, Suffolk)

Juliette Wade 18–19 (Alderley Grange, Gloucestershire), 40 (Mrs S. Brooke, Overstroud Cottage, Great Missenden, Buckinghamshire), 122, 133 (Dr and Mrs A. J. Cox, Woodpeckers, Marlcliff, Warwickshire)